A Note From Denise Renner

The Word of God is so powerful in our lives. It is essential that every person spend time with God and study His Word in order to stay spiritually strong in these last days.

This study guide corresponds to my *TIME With Denise Renner* TV program by the same title that can be viewed at **deniserenner.org**. My desire is that through these lessons, you find the encouragement and freedom in Christ that you need. I believe the Holy Spirit is going to speak to you through the words you read in this study tool and that as you begin to use it, you will be *propelled* into the abundant life God has planned for you. I encourage you to make the effort to receive all He has for you and all He wants to do in you — it will definitely be worth it!

Whether you have walked with the Lord a long time or have just begun to follow Him, there is so much He wants to give you from His Word. He sees where you are, and He wants to meet you there.

> Therefore do not worry about tomorrow, for tomorrow
> will worry about its own things.
> Sufficient for the day is its own trouble.
> — Matthew 6:34

Your sister and friend in Jesus Christ,

Denise Renner

Denise Renner

Unless otherwise indicated, all scripture quotations are taken from the *New King James Version*®. Copyright © 1982 by Thomas Nelson. Used by permission. All rights reserved.

Scripture quotations marked (*KJV*) are taken from the *King James Version* of the Bible.

The Supply Inside You

Copyright © 2024 by Denise Renner
1814 W. Tacoma St.
Broken Arrow, Oklahoma 74012-1406

Published by Rick Renner Ministries
www.renner.org

ISBN 13: 978-1-6675-1102-3

ISBN 13 eBook: 978-1-6675-1103-0

All rights reserved. No portion of this book may be reproduced or transmitted in any form or by any means — electronic, mechanical, photocopy, recording, scanning, or other (except for brief quotations in critical reviews or articles) — without the prior written permission of the Publisher.

LESSON 1

TOPIC
You Have a Supply

SCRIPTURES

1. **Ephesians 4:16** — From whom the whole body, joined and knit together by what every joint supplies, according to the effective working by which every part does its share, causes growth of the body for the edifying of itself in love.
2. **Philippians 1:6** — Being confident of this very thing, that He who has begun a good work in you will complete it until the day of Jesus Christ.
3. **2 Corinthians 10:12** — For we dare not class ourselves or compare ourselves with those who commend themselves. But they, measuring themselves by themselves, and comparing themselves among themselves, are not wise.
4. **Philemon 1:6** — That the sharing of your faith may become effective by the acknowledgment of every good thing which is in you in Christ Jesus.
5. **Ephesians 4:24** — And that you put on the new man which was created according to God, in true righteousness and holiness.
6. **1 Corinthians 6:19** — Or do you not know that your body is the temple of the Holy Spirit who is in you, whom you have from God, and you are not your own?
7. **Hebrews 11:24-27** — By faith Moses, when he became of age, refused to be called the son of Pharaoh's daughter, choosing rather to suffer affliction with the people of God than to enjoy the passing pleasures of sin, esteeming the reproach of Christ greater riches than the treasures in Egypt; for he looked to the reward. By faith he forsook Egypt, not fearing the wrath of the king; for he endured as seeing Him who is invisible.

SYNOPSIS

The ten lessons in this study on *The Supply Inside You* will focus on the following topics:

- You Have a Supply
- Keep Moving Forward
- Overcoming Rejection
- The Power of Forgiveness
- Turning Away From Negative Opinions
- Victory in Agreeing With God
- Getting Past the Voices of Others
- Faith for a Miracle
- It Is Well
- A Greater Purpose

The power and supply of the Holy Spirit are on the inside of you, and your partnership with Him is an *unstoppable* force against any pressures the devil or this world can bring. When you align yourself with the Spirit of God, you find your place in the Body of Christ and begin to walk in the power that only He can supply. In this lesson, Denise reveals how the supply of the Holy Spirit manifests as each part of the Body partners with Him to bring a unique supply. When all the joints work together, the Body of Christ is able to move in great power, victory, and unity!

The emphasis of this lesson:

Like a physical body, the Body of Christ is composed of a variety of different joints, each carrying a unique supply that benefits the whole. God designed each of us with a special grace and anointing to carry out a work within the Body. However, the enemy delights in hindering our supply by bringing thoughts of comparison, accusation, and low self-esteem. To stand against his attacks, we must fight using the Word of God. By acknowledging all the good things God has placed in us by Christ Jesus, we can walk free of the enemy's accusations and release the magnificent supply inside us!

Comparison Is Unwise

After Jesus died, was buried, was raised to life, and sat down at the right hand of God, He no longer had a physical body present on this earth. But the good news is, He has called *us* — the Church — to be His Body! If you're a believer, you are a valuable member of the Body of Christ.

Ephesians 4:16 says, "From whom the whole body, joined and knit together by what every joint supplies, according to the effective working by which every part does its share, causes growth of the body for the edifying of itself in love." No matter who you are or what you do, you are a "joint"— a connecting piece in the Body of Christ — and you must recognize that you have a unique and supernatural supply of the Holy Spirit inside you that others in the Body need.

Recognizing the supply of the Spirit that is in you begins with acknowledging all the good things God has done in you through Christ Jesus (*see* Philemon 1:6). Not only has Jesus saved you, redeemed you, and set you free from sin, but He has also given you the Holy Spirit as your Great Helper. He has placed unique gifts and abilities in you and graced you to fulfill His plan and live in a way that glorifies Him. The good things He has placed in you are wonderful, deep, and magnificent!

However, if you begin to compare yourself to others, the joy that comes from acknowledging all the good things God has placed in you will quickly dissipate. In fact, the Bible warns us not to compare ourselves with others:

> **For we dare not class ourselves or compare ourselves with those who commend themselves. But they, measuring themselves by themselves, and comparing themselves among themselves, are not wise.**
> **— 2 Corinthians 10:12**

Comparison can cause you to fall into many errors including pride, competition, low self-esteem, jealousy, envy, and covetousness. It can also distract you from the race God has called you to run and hinder you from freely giving your supply to the rest of the Body of Christ.

On the program, Denise shared about a time in her life when she compared herself to her husband Rick and the effect it had on her. Over the course of their years in ministry, Denise often traveled with Rick, and she always had a front-row seat in his meetings. She watched as he powerfully preached the Word of God night after night. Anytime he preached, people's lives were touched and changed for the better. And even though Denise was thankful for the ministry of the Holy Spirit through Rick, she still found herself comparing herself to him. According to Second Corinthians 10:12, she was being *unwise*.

As Denise began to compare herself to her husband, she started to see herself as "less" than him. In her own eyes, she paled in the shadow of Rick's great influence and effectiveness in ministry. But those thoughts were *not* God's will for Denise! She didn't realize that she was a unique joint in the Body of Christ with a unique supply to give. God had placed specific gifts and abilities in Denise, but the enemy had successfully used shame and insecurity to convince her to hold back her supply. She was unknowingly putting down and minimizing the supply God had uniquely given her.

You're a Joint and You Have a Supply!

The human body has hundreds of joints, and each one is extremely important. Many people exercise and take supplements specifically to maintain their joint health. And if you've ever experienced joint *pain*, you know that when even one joint suffers, the whole body is affected. The relationship between a body and its joints so beautifully illustrates the way believers in the Church are connected. You are a joint in the Body of Christ, and what's in you affects the rest of the Body! Your supply is vital for someone else. But if you believe the lies of comparison, sadly, you will deprive the rest of the Body of your unique supply that only you can give.

On the program, Denise shared about another time she compared herself to someone else. Often when Rick and Denise travel and minister around the United States, they meet many different pastors and their spouses. On one particular trip, Denise met a pastor's wife who was kind, industrious, a wonderful mother, and a great homemaker. She homeschooled her children, grew a garden, made rugs, and even canned her own food! To Denise, she was the epitome of a Proverbs 31 woman.

Even though this sweet pastor's wife was extremely loving to Denise and didn't do anything unkind to her, Denise felt insecure and saw herself as inferior to this woman. The enemy began to accuse Denise, whispering thoughts like, *You need to be more like her*, and, *You aren't as good as she is.* Again, Denise was being *unwise*.

Finally, Denise caught on to the devil's scheme and corrected her perspective. She stopped comparing herself to this sweet lady and began to acknowledge the good things God had put in her. As a result, Denise's flow of supply was not hindered in the Body.

To delve further into the subject of comparison, Denise shared this excerpt from her book *Unstoppable*:

> When we compare ourselves with others, we actually do give place to the voice of the accuser. It is as if we join hands with him and say in our soul, *Okay, Satan, tell me more about how I don't measure up. Explain to me again why what I have to give is not valuable.*
>
> Does that scenario sound familiar? Have you ever let negative thoughts erase and diminish all the good that you have to give? If so, you need to remember this: The devil is never, ever going to say to you, *Oh, you are doing such a great job! You are bringing so much glory to Jesus in helping others. Keep going!*
>
> However, the enemy *will* say, *Don't give what you have, because it's not as good as what those people have. They already have their supply. That's enough. They don't need yours.*

Have you ever heard those horrible, lying words? The truth is, those words were spoken to you by the devil to stop you and get you to lay down what God has placed inside you. The enemy is *so intimidated* by the call of God on your life, your born-again spirit, the love of God in your heart, and the supply of God in you that he wants to stop you from giving what you have. The devil will go to great lengths to tempt, accuse, distract, and torment you. But don't give in to his tactics! Acknowledge the good things in you and rejoice in where God has placed you in the Body. Your supply is significant!

Your Supply Is Inside

As you seek to know more about your supply in the Body, it's important that you first recognize the supply comes from the new life *inside* you. It's not based on outward appearances but on the person of the heart. Ephesians 4:24 admonishes believers to "put on the new man which was created according to God, in true righteousness and holiness." When you were born again, the Holy Spirit came into your spirit and brought God's righteousness and holiness with it. On the inside, you look just like Jesus! It's this very essence of Jesus inside you that terrifies the devil.

You may be thinking, *Sure, this power is available to preachers or pulpit ministers, but are you really saying that this is available to me?* YES! This power is for *every* believer — not just ministers — and that includes you. Because the Holy Spirit lives in you, you can be confident that His power is also present within you.

God's Word constantly reminds us of the indwelling presence of the Holy Spirit. For example, First Corinthians 6:19 states, "Or do you not know that your body is the temple of the Holy Spirit who is in you, whom you have from God, and you are not your own?" According to this verse, the Holy Spirit lives *in* every believer!

Did you know that you are more than your physical body? Your body is just the outward shell that houses your spirit, which is inhabited by the Spirit of God. You are more than what you see when you look in the mirror or your physical description — your height, weight, hair color, skin color, and eye color. Your true nature — the *real* you — is your magnificent, born-again, recreated spirit on the inside, where the Holy Spirit resides.

Esteeming the Spiritual Treasures Within

In Hebrews 11:24-27, we see an Old Testament example of someone who was so focused on eternal things — on things unseen — that he forsook the temporal riches of the world, rejecting them by comparison because he was so captivated by the promise of a future, heavenly reward.

> **By faith Moses, when he became of age, refused to be called the son of Pharaoh's daughter, choosing rather to suffer affliction with the people of God than to enjoy the passing pleasures of sin, esteeming the reproach of Christ greater riches than the treasures in Egypt; for he looked to the reward. By faith he forsook Egypt, not fearing the wrath of the king; for he endured as seeing Him who is invisible.**

At that time in history, the treasures in Egypt were the greatest treasures known to man! But even though leaving the household of Pharaoh would cost Moses something in the natural, it didn't even compare to the rewards, both in this life and the one to come, that he knew God had in store for him and the nation of Israel. Moses could confidently sacrifice what was naturally valuable because he had set his sights on something far deeper and greater and *saw Him who is invisible* (*see* v. 27).

In the same way, it takes faith to see what God put on the inside of us. It's an invisible supply, but it certainly exists! And the more we release our faith, the more all those good things will become a reality to us and become a blessing to those around us. They are a treasure to God, and we need to see them as a treasure too!

On the program, Denise shared this testimony of how she came to value the treasure on the inside of her:

> Many years ago, Rick was teaching on Hebrews 11:24-27, and as he was teaching, I thought, *Oh Father! I have such a treasure on the inside of me! It's greater than any riches on the outside.*
>
> Before that day, I had been struggling with comparing myself to my sister because she had a great job, and Rick and I were barely surviving! Our financial situation was so bad that we needed supernatural help. Many people had mercy on us and gave us food to eat and even bought clothes for our children. We were in a bad place!
>
> But as Rick taught on Hebrews 11:24-27 that day, I started thinking about the treasure on the inside of me. Later that afternoon, we went to my mother's house and my sister was there. I usually compared myself to her and thought, *Oh, I'm not as good as she is; I'm not as beautiful; I don't have as much as she has.* But that day, I was so aware of the treasure inside me that I walked in there with my shoulders back, and I was filled with confidence and joy. I wasn't looking at what she had on the outside — I was looking at what *I* had on the *inside*.

If you're struggling with confidence, it's time for you to recognize all that God has placed in you. This inside treasure is more valuable than diamonds, gold, or earthly riches. When you understand your spiritual value, you can stand with your shoulders back and head held high. The riches of Christ are unsearchable — and they're inside you!

When you focus on your external appearance or circumstances, you are seeing that which is temporal or temporary. But when you focus on the work God has done in you, you are seeing that which is eternal, and you see the truth of who you really are in Christ. You must acknowledge the supply of the Spirit in you, the love of God in your heart, and the resurrection power that flows through your spirit because what you have to give will touch the people around you and change their lives.

There's nothing more magnificent than the indwelling resurrection power of Christ. Once you gain a revelation of that power, nothing can stop you. This truth has the ability to vanquish condemnation, self-doubt, pride, and arrogance. You have a treasure inside, and it's the life of Jesus flowing within you!

Philippians 1:6 says, "Being confident of this very thing, that He who has begun a good work in you will complete it until the day of Jesus Christ." That means the Holy Spirit is helping you recognize your supply and teaching you how to release it. His grace is always with you to reveal to you your individual assignment and to provide you with the power to fulfill it. That's why you can boldly say, "I am a joint, and I have a supply. I agree with the Holy Spirit to do my part and to release this treasure He has placed within me!"

Friend, your confidence in the power of God has the potential to unlock your supply. If you will acknowledge all those good things in you by Christ Jesus (*see* Philemon 6) and look to the invisible realm through the eyes of faith (*see* Hebrews 11:24-27), you can begin to release that powerful flow inside you to others. You are a joint, and you have a magnificent supply to offer the Body of Christ!

STUDY QUESTIONS

Be diligent to present yourself approved to God, a worker who does not need to be ashamed, rightly dividing the word of truth.
— 2 Timothy 2:15

1. Ephesians 4:16 says, "From whom the whole body, joined and knit together by what every joint supplies, according to the effective working by which every part does its share, causes growth of the body for the edifying of itself in love." What did the apostle Paul mean in this verse when he referred to believers as "joints" in the Body of Christ?
2. Read First Corinthians 6:19 and then review the section in this lesson titled "Your Supply Is Inside." How does this shape how you see yourself? Take a moment and describe the *real* you.
3. Second Corinthians 10:12 says, "For we dare not class ourselves or compare ourselves with those who commend themselves. But they,

measuring themselves by themselves, and comparing themselves among themselves, are not wise." According to this verse, how would you describe the person who compares himself or herself to someone else? What advice or counsel could you give that person to help set him or her free from the trap of comparison?

PRACTICAL APPLICATION

> But be doers of the word,
> and not hearers only, deceiving yourselves.
> —James 1:22

1. Philemon 1:6 says, "That the sharing of your faith may become effective by the acknowledgment of every good thing which is in you in Christ Jesus." Take a moment to acknowledge and reflect on all the good things God has put in you by Christ Jesus. List three qualities that stand out to you the most. How have you stewarded or nurtured those things, and how will you better use them to serve the Body of Christ this week?
2. Think of a time when you compared yourself to others and felt inadequate. How did this affect your ability to serve others with the gifts inside you? Now think of someone you know who has struggled with thoughts of inadequacy. What scriptures and personal testimonies can you share to encourage that person to give his or her supply?
3. Read Hebrews 11:24-27. Moses chose to value and prioritize the eternal treasure in him over what he saw in the natural. What are some temporary things in your life that you tend to focus on, such as external appearance or circumstances? In what ways will you shift your focus to eternal things and better steward the gifts God has put inside you?

LESSON 2

TOPIC
Keep Moving Forward

SCRIPTURES
1. **Philemon 1:6** — That the sharing of your faith may become effective by the acknowledgment of every good thing which is in you in Christ Jesus.
2. **Philippians 3:12,13** — Not that I have already attained, or am already perfected; but I press on, that I may lay hold of that for which Christ Jesus has also laid hold of me. Brethren, I do not count myself to have apprehended; but one thing I do, forgetting those things which are behind and reaching forward to those things which are ahead.
3. **Luke 5:36-39** — Then He spoke a parable to them: "No one puts a piece from a new garment on an old one; otherwise the new makes a tear, and also the piece that was taken out of the new does not match the old. And no one puts new wine into old wineskins; or else the new wine will burst the wineskins and be spilled, and the wineskins will be ruined. But new wine must be put into the new wineskins, and both are preserved. And no one, having drunk old wine, immediately desires new; for he says, 'The old is better.'"

SYNOPSIS
Letting go of the past and moving forward into the bright future God has in store for us can be challenging. But by relinquishing the voices, habits, patterns, and mindsets of the past, we can receive God's new wine for a brand-new season in our life. In this lesson, we will discuss another hindrance to the free-flowing, supernatural power of God in our lives — holding on to the past.

The emphasis of this lesson:

Refusing to let go of the past can cause many problems in the Body of Christ and hinder each of us from moving forward into the next season of God's plans. In order to release the old, we must relinquish the voices of the past that may have condemned or criticized us. By allowing the

Holy Spirit to work deep inside our hearts, we can overcome the disappointments, hurts, wounds, and challenges of previous seasons and move forward into our future. God desires to pour new wine into all of us, but it requires our cooperation with Him to receive the new changes He wants to accomplish in us.

In the first lesson, Denise shared about the amazing power in being a "joint" in the Body of Christ. There is a unique supply of the Holy Spirit on the inside of you, and people are just waiting to receive it. Many people in the world are suffering without hope because they don't have Christ (*see* Ephesians 2:12), but we have so much we can offer them. The love of God, His supernatural hope, and the resurrection power that is in us by the Holy Spirit are *exactly* what people need!

Philemon 1:6 says, "That the sharing of your faith may become effective by the acknowledgment of every good thing which is in you in Christ Jesus." It is our responsibility to acknowledge what God has put inside each of us. And when we do, we'll see the supernatural supply of the Spirit begin to flow out from our spirit to the people around us.

But if we're not careful, we may find ourselves comparing our supply to someone else's. This is dangerous because it not only causes us to shy away from the call of God on our lives, but it deprives others of the unique supply of God that should be flowing from us. Instead, we need to push the voices of others and the voice of our past aside and reach forward for what God has for us!

Walking Free From the Past

Has the voice of the past ever tried to speak to you about a mistake you made or something someone else did to hurt you? One obstacle that may try to stop you in life is the voice of the past. But it *must* be silenced, because if you listen to that voice long enough, it has the power to hinder you from running your race.

One of the greatest examples of leaving the past behind is the apostle Paul. Before his encounter with Jesus, he was a terror to the Church. He threatened Christians, beat them, imprisoned them, hunted them down, and killed them. Just imagine what thoughts must have come to his mind after he turned his life around.

Paul might have dealt with thoughts like, *You killed Christians, and you enjoyed their suffering. You're not worthy to preach the Gospel!* We don't know exactly what thoughts came to his mind or what temptations he was faced with, but we do know he had been lied about, stolen from, betrayed, and persecuted. He could have spent his time dwelling on the past or on what others had done to him. He could have entertained thoughts such as, *Oh, poor me!* But, instead, Paul chose to forget the past and move *forward*.

Philippians 3:12 and 13 says,

> **Not that I have already attained, or am already perfected; but I press on, that I may lay hold of that for which Christ Jesus has also laid hold of me. Brethren, I do not count myself to have apprehended; but one thing I do, forgetting those things which are behind and reaching forward to those things which are ahead.**

When Paul said in verse 13, "…one thing I do…," he was emphasizing what was coming next. He really wanted the Philippian church to recognize and pay attention to the powerful statement he said next — Paul let go of the past and *reached forward* toward the future.

When Paul met Jesus on the road to Damascus, his heart was changed. He was washed clean of all the horrible things he had done to people, and the new life of Jesus came into his heart and transformed him from the inside out. No longer a murderer, Paul became one of the greatest proponents for Christ in the entire Church.

It is because of this great revelation of the redeeming work of Christ that Paul could pen the words in Philippians 3:12 and 13. Instead of fixating on the errors of his past, he chose to focus on the future God had in store for him. He was pressing forward with all his might to finish his race and win the prize.

Historians say that at the time the apostle Paul wrote the book of Philippians, he was imprisoned in a Roman jail. He was standing in a cell filled with sewage, darkness, and filth. This was a place where hope died — yet Paul wasn't moved by these hopeless circumstances. He spent his days rejoicing and praising God! In that hopeless prison and from a persevering heart, Paul wrote to the Philippian church about leaving the past behind and pushing forward to the future. *Wow!*

Considering all that Paul had been through, it would have been easier for him to give up and die so he could be with the Lord and thus put an end to his suffering. He even said in Philippians 1:21 "For to me, to live is Christ, and to die is gain." But then in verse 24 he said, "Nevertheless to remain in the flesh is more needful for you." He pushed past the painful, torturous present he was in and the thoughts that were likely bombarding his mind and took hold of the future God had in store for him. And his letter to the Philippian church encouraged other believers to do the same regardless of their own personal circumstances.

Paul determined in his heart to take hold of the things God had provided for him. He wasn't going to give up in the middle of that deep, dark jail cell. He was acknowledging God and all the good things Christ had done in him. The more he continued to rejoice, the more faith rose inside him. He wasn't going to let the accusatory thoughts about what he had done in his past or the perceived hopelessness of his present circumstances shake his confidence in the plans God still had for him and for his future.

As a result of Paul's tenacity to put the past behind and press forward for the future, the devil could not keep him bound. Paul stayed in the fight and refused to let fear, depression, or anxiety overcome him. He continued rejoicing in God's faithfulness until, one day, those prison chains were loosed, and he was set free!

Take Hold!

Again, Philippians 3:12 says, "Not that I have already attained, or am already perfected; but I press on, that I may lay hold of that for which Christ Jesus has also laid hold of me." He wanted to take hold of what Christ Jesus had laid hold of him for. Have you taken hold of the things that God has provided for you? He wants you to have supernatural experiences with Him, He wants you to learn about the power and authority that you have in Christ, and He wants you to experience the love of God more and more. But, like the apostle Paul, you must press forward and leave the past behind.

There is so much about God to be discovered! Paul was a powerful minister of the Gospel who wrote two-thirds of the New Testament, but even he wasn't able to press so far forward that he knew everything there was to know about God. No, he said in Philippians 3:13, "Brethren, I do not count myself to have apprehended...." He didn't know it all, but he did *do* one thing. He forgot those things which were behind and reached forward to those things which were ahead. God had grabbed hold of Paul, and in response, he reached forward and grabbed hold of the very thing he was placed on this earth to do.

What a holy thing it is to acknowledge the hold that God has on you! If you're a believer, then you were bought with a price — the precious blood of Christ (*see* 1 Corinthians 6:20). The Bible says in John 15:16 that He chose you; you didn't choose Him. That means He saw you, chose you, and paid the highest price that could be paid to snatch you out of hell's grasp and pull you out of a destructive, empty, hopeless life. He apprehended you from that dark future and gave you a new, glorious future to reach toward.

God has things in store for your future that you don't even know about. His plans for you are always good (*see* Jeremiah 29:11). He wants to pour Himself out on you so that you can know even more about Him by the Holy Spirit living on the inside of you. But in order to walk in those things, you must use your faith to say "goodbye" to the past and take hold of the future He has for you!

New Wine in New Wineskins

In Luke 5:36-39, Jesus tells an interesting parable about new garments and new wineskins:

> **…No one puts a piece from a new garment on an old one; otherwise the new makes a tear, and also the piece that was taken out of the new does not match the old. And no one puts new wine into old wineskins; or else the new wine will burst the wineskins and be spilled, and the wineskins will be ruined. But new wine must be put into new wineskins, and both are preserved. And no one, having drunk old wine, immediately desires new; for he says, 'The old is better.'**

Jesus is painting a picture of what it's like to move forward from the old into the new. He describes how incompatible our past is with our future and powerfully reveals the truth about pushing forward. When you refuse to let go of the old, you become like an old piece of garment that tears up the new work God wants to do in your life. You become like an old wineskin that can't receive the new wine. You must come into agreement with the new things God wants to pour forth into your life.

He's calling you further into Him, but your stubbornness to cooperate with Him can cause damage not only to yourself but to others around you. Don't choose to remain in the comfort of the familiar because of fear of the new and exciting things God has in store for you. His plans are always good, and you don't need to fear the unknown when it comes to God's plan for your life.

Letting Go of the Old To Receive the New

Once you've made a decision to leave the old behind and press on toward the new, you may find that the people around you are still focused on the old. You may also find that some people who have been used to the old are not necessarily happy for you as you begin to step into the new things God has planned.

You may hear comments like, "You'll never change; I've seen your bad habits," or "I know you'll fail. You failed last time!" These people only see the old wine. But don't let their stubbornness keep you from following after God's will. God has *new wine* for you, and it is not compatible with the old wineskins of the past. You must make a decision to receive what God has in store *no matter what*.

But in order to receive God's new wine, you must let go of the old. This may require you to relinquish old mindsets, bad habits, and negative opinions of others. You might have believed one thing about yourself before, but when you see yourself in the new light of God's Word, you have to allow your thoughts to conform to the new. You have to push past the difficulties and fear of failure. Although you might have fallen last time, you can get up and push forward! You can press into the bright future God has set for you.

You may be used to your old patterns, habits, or traditions. But when the Lord begins to deal with you about changes in your life, it is important that you remain willing to receive what He has for you in the new season. You can say, "Yes, Lord. I agree with your new wine. I receive it. I know this is going to stretch me, but I'm going to grab hold of the new wine you want to pour in me."

Regardless of what God wants to do in you, you must realize you can't live in the past and take hold of the future at the same time. The old and the new don't mix, just like new patches don't work on an old garment. When you try to mix the two, you will create tears that end up destroying the whole garment altogether.

Thankfully, the Holy Spirit is in you to help you make the necessary changes you need. You are not alone in this transition because the Holy Spirit lives on the inside of you. He can help you get rid of the old garment and take hold of the new.

Denise wrote about the help of the Holy Spirit, and in the program, she shared the following excerpt from her book, *Unstoppable*:

> Sometimes there are those who do come alongside to encourage us along the way, and that's so wonderful when it happens. But even then, no one is with us 24/7 — and no one is perfect. Many times when it's the midnight hour, it's just us and the Holy Spirit. But aren't we thankful we have Him, the perfect Helper! The Holy Spirit will join with us as we seek Him for our needed supply of the new wine of His presence and His plan for the days ahead. It simply takes our heart decision to open up and receive His help. He has exactly what we need at all times and seasons.

No matter what challenges may have been in your past, you can rise above them through the power of the Spirit. If your current circumstances are challenging, you can rejoice through them just like the apostle Paul. The temptations, failures, and opinions of the past don't have to keep you fettered to a closed chapter. You can set your sights on the future and receive God's new wine!

STUDY QUESTIONS

Be diligent to present yourself approved to God, a worker who does not need to be ashamed, rightly dividing the word of truth.
— 2 Timothy 2:15

1. According to Paul's example in Philippians 3:12 and 13, Paul responded to thoughts about his past by letting them go and focusing on what was ahead instead. In what ways does Philippians 1:21-24 show Paul's commitment to pressing forward in God's purpose for his life, even in the face of suffering and hardship?
2. Explain what Jesus meant when He said in Luke 5:36, "…No one puts a piece from a new garment on an old one; otherwise the new

makes a tear, and also the piece that was taken out of the new does not match the old."
3. Philippians 3:12 and 13 says, "Not that I have already attained, or am already perfected; but I press on, that I may lay hold of that for which Christ Jesus has also laid hold of me. Brethren, I do not count myself to have apprehended; but one thing I do, forgetting those things which are behind and reaching forward to those things which are ahead." Now read John 14:15-18. Describe the Holy Spirit's role in a believer's process of letting go of the past and pressing on toward what is ahead.

PRACTICAL APPLICATION

> But be doers of the word,
> and not hearers only, deceiving yourselves.
> —James 1:22

1. How have past mistakes, criticism from others, or hurtful experiences influenced your self-perception? In what ways have these voices tried to hold you back from fully embracing your identity in Christ?
2. What changes will you make to ensure God's opinion of you remains your focus as you pursue His plan for your life? How does Philippians 1:21-24 encourage you to keep pressing forward?
3. Paul went from being a persecutor of Christians to being the most influential apostle in the history of our faith. In what ways does Paul's transformation on the road to Damascus demonstrate the power of grace and forgiveness? How does Paul's story inspire you to view your past mistakes or shortcomings?
4. Read Jeremiah 29:11. What does it mean to you that God has good plans for your life? How can you actively seek to understand and embrace those plans while letting go of past burdens? What areas of your life has God been dealing with you to change?

LESSON 3

TOPIC
Overcoming Rejection

SCRIPTURES
1. **Hebrews 12:1** — Therefore we also, since we are surrounded by so great a cloud of witnesses, let us lay aside every weight, and the sin which so easily ensnares us, and let us run with endurance the race that is set before us.
2. **John 3:16** — For God so loved the world that He gave His only begotten Son, that whoever believes in Him should not perish but have everlasting life.
3. **2 Timothy 4:7,8** — I have fought the good fight, I have finished the race, I have kept the faith. Finally, there is laid up for me the crown of righteousness, which the Lord, the righteous Judge, will give to me on that Day, and not to me only but also to all who have loved His appearing.
4. **2 Peter 1:14** *(KJV)* — "…Shortly I must put off this my tabernacle.…"

SYNOPSIS
In this lesson, Denise addresses the damage unforgiveness and rejection can bring to a person's mental and physical health. By understanding God's love, believers have a powerful tool to overcome rejection and run their race unhindered by the weights of unforgiveness.

The emphasis of this lesson:

Harboring unforgiveness in our hearts can cause us to wither inside and withhold our supply from the Body of Christ. If we don't deal with unforgiveness, it can even affect the wellbeing of our minds, bodies, and souls. Thankfully, we have a supernatural remedy — the divine love of God — that lives on the inside of us. When we choose to release this love, we can walk free from the hurt, pain, and damage caused by the words or actions of others. We don't have to be a victim in this life; instead, we can become a victor by choosing to walk in the love of Christ.

In previous lessons, we learned about the amazing power of being a "joint" in the Body of Christ, the destructive nature of comparison, and how letting go of the past frees us to walk in the hope of God's plans for our future. And as we utilize these tools, we will become even more effective in giving from our unique supply of the Holy Spirit's power that God has put in us.

We are called to be conduits of God's supernatural life and the power of His Spirit; however, for this supernatural power to flow freely in and through us, we must also address the hindrances that keep us from fully walking in the freedom God has for us.

Unforgiveness Can Affect Your Health

As we continue to examine how to give from the unique supply God has given us, it is important to monitor the health of our own heart. Forgiveness is a powerful force that keeps us moving forward in spite of hurt, offense, or difficulty, but on the other hand, unforgiveness can poison our supply and hinder us from accomplishing God's plan for our lives. If we want to remain unstoppable and give from our supply freely, we must learn to forgive others just as Christ has forgiven us.

Unforgiveness, bitterness, and rejection are powerful emotions that can imprison our hearts, attitudes, thoughts, actions, and behaviors. They can destroy relationships and stop us from giving what God has placed inside us to give to others. If not released to the Lord, these damaging emotions can even cause us to become sick in our bodies.

On the program, Denise shared a personal testimony from a time in her life when God helped her walk free of unforgiveness and the effects it had on her physical body. For two years, Denise had been experiencing a strange phenomenon in her extremities. Her hands and feet were painfully cold all the time. She was also tremendously fearful and experienced tormenting thoughts that resulted in debilitating panic attacks. Her physical condition and mental torment were so severe that Denise sought God's direction and determined that she would not stop seeking until she heard from God.

One day, the Lord showed her the reality of her situation: she had been harboring unforgiveness in her heart toward someone, and she didn't even know it! The bitterness she had been holding on to was having a very real, physical effect on her body. When she realized that unforgiveness had taken root in her heart and was causing her to become sick, she repented before God, forgave the person she had been holding a grudge against, and even asked that person for forgiveness.

That night, as Denise slept, Jesus performed a miracle in her heart! When she awoke the next morning, she felt as if an invisible hand had reached down into her heart and pulled out all the tentacles of pain that bitterness and unforgiveness had brought to her soul. It was as if she was now in a completely different world than the one she had been living in for the last two years. She was completely delivered!

From that moment on, the cold sensation in Denise's hands and feet stopped, the panic attacks ceased, and the tormenting thoughts dissipated. It was forgiveness that opened the door for Jesus to come in and do the miraculous work of expelling the rejection and unforgiveness from her heart. Because she allowed God's love to wash over her, Denise became free from all the anguish that unforgiveness had produced in her life.

You Have the Choice To Forgive

God's love is so powerful! It's greater than all the bitterness and unforgiveness inside a person. It is that very same love that took Jesus to the Cross, and it has the power to extinguish rejection — and the fear and torment associated with it.

Many times in the gospels, Jesus commands us to forgive because He knows it is tempting for us to respond to rejection with unforgiveness, bitterness, or resentfulness. Offenses will come, but we will always have the opportunity to choose between the bondage of bitterness and the freedom of forgiveness.

On the program, Denise shared another story of a woman who had been diagnosed with cancer and experienced the negative effects of unforgiveness on her physical health. After this woman was diagnosed, she asked a particular minister to pray for her. And as he prayed in tongues, she began speaking out, listing every time she she'd ever experienced deep rejection from someone. She said things like, "Oh, this person left me! That person left me!" And as she began to let go of all the bitterness and unforgiveness that often accompanies rejection, something supernatural happened. Her body was completely healed of cancer!

As time went on, this woman again experienced a deep rejection from someone she loved, and sadly, that cancer came right back into her body. When she experienced that rejection, she was presented with a choice to make. She could respond with bitterness and unforgiveness or she could choose to forgive. Unfortunately, she chose the path of resentment and unforgiveness, and the woman eventually died.

Our bodies were not made to carry rejection and hurt. In fact, an article from Johns Hopkins Medicine reports that the act of forgiving has many benefits for a person's health.[1] It can lower the risk of a heart attack, improve cholesterol levels, aid in better sleep, reduce pain, and lower blood pressure. It has even been shown to reduce levels of depression, stress, and anxiety. While being in a state of unforgiveness or anger can incite a person's fight or flight response, causing a whole load of problems, forgiveness has just the opposite effect. It calms stress levels and leads to improved health.

When we don't forgive, we open the door for disease to come into our bodies. And medical science is confirming what the Bible has been telling us all along — we must forgive others as Christ has forgiven us. There is health, healing, and longevity in forgiveness!

Love Extinguishes Rejection

Jesus says that we must forgive others so that God will forgive us (*see* Matthew 6:14). And the Bible instructs us to lay aside the weight of rejection, bitterness, and unforgiveness so that we can run our race effectively. If we hang on to these weights, they will trip us up and hinder us in our walk with God.

Hebrews 12:1 says:

> **Therefore we also, since we are surrounded by so great a cloud of witnesses, let us lay aside every weight, and the sin which so easily ensnares us, and let us run with endurance the race that is set before us.**

Jesus was rejected (*see* Isaiah 53:3; John 1:10,11), so He knows what it's like to be hurt by someone you deeply love. It can be very painful. Jesus was even rejected by *God* when He hung on the Cross (*see* Matthew 27:46). But because of His sacrifice, we can be free from the damaging effects of rejection by forgiving those who hurt us. Forgiveness is the great expeller of rejection! Jesus loved those who hurt Him and overcame the horrible evil of mankind — and mankind was forgiven.

Thankfully, God has provided the tool of forgiveness, which is the power that quells unforgiveness. This power dwells on the inside of us through the new birth, and it is the same love that was present in Jesus when He went to the Cross. John 3:16 says, "For God so loved the world that He gave His only begotten Son, that whoever believes in Him should not perish but have everlasting life."

The supernatural love of God was on display when Jesus gave His life on the Cross. Our God came into the world and took upon Himself our sin, unforgiveness, guilt, and shame, and set us free. He paid the price for our judgment, and only this kind of love has the power to free us from rejection and unforgiveness. There is nothing more powerful on this earth than the love of God — and that love is in you. Therefore, the power to forgive others is in you.

Rejection, if embraced, can leave you as a victim. But you don't have to be the victim anymore. Jesus paid the price for every part of your heart to be free from rejection, pain, and unforgiveness. Through Christ, you can rise up in freedom, release forgiveness, and become a victor!

Forgiveness Takes You From 'Victim' to Victor!

An example of someone who chose to walk in this type of forgiveness was the apostle Paul. The Bible records the many sufferings he experienced in his ministry — he was robbed, betrayed, persecuted, and lied about, but he didn't die a victim. Paul might have been a martyr, but he died a *victor*. In fact, Paul wrote in Second Timothy 4:7 and 8:

> **I have fought the good fight, I have finished the race, I have kept the faith. Finally, there is laid up for me the crown of righteousness, which the Lord, the righteous Judge, will give to me on that Day, and not to me only but also to all who have loved His appearing.**

Because Paul embraced the power of forgiveness, he was able to release all those who had beaten him, persecuted him, or betrayed him. At the end of his life, he wasn't a bitter man or a broken victim. He was full of the love of God, which kept him free from hating all those who had hurt him.

On the program, Denise shared about the time she visited the city of Rome and saw the place where, according to historians, the apostle Paul was decapitated. History tells us that the guards didn't need to force or drag Paul to the tree stump where they would take his life. He actually *ran toward* it and *embraced* it and then *willingly* positioned himself to be decapitated. Paul even described his coming death in Second Peter 1:14 (*KJV*), saying, "…Shortly I must put off this my tabernacle."

Despite the fact that Paul was going to die at the hands of these people, he didn't allow bitterness to settle in his heart. Paul allowed the power and presence of the Holy Spirit in him and the love that had been shed abroad in his heart to flow from his spirit and extinguish all the pain of rejection — and he finished his race with *joy* (*see* Acts 20:24).

The love of God is greater than any hate, hurt, anger, or offense. It's more powerful than any assault or damage someone might have inflicted against you. This supernatural love flows from the life of God through your spirit. It's the same love that Jesus had for those who crucified Him. Even though these people had spit on Him, beat Him, and rejected Him, Jesus was still able to speak the words recorded in Luke 23:34: "…Father, forgive them, for they do not know what they do…."

This amazing love is the great extinguisher of rejection. Although you might feel intense pain from the hurtful words or actions of others, God's love inside you is louder than those voices. The devil may lie to you and say, "You're not good enough. You're not wanted." But that's not what Jesus says. Jesus says you're accepted in the beloved! (*See* Ephesians 1:6.) Let God's love bubble up from the inside of you and drown out those thoughts of fear, defeat, or intimidation.

It doesn't matter if someone has rejected you, lied about you, or made fun of you. You are loved in Christ! Those words of rejection might have pierced your soul, but you can release the people who hurt you to the Lord and continue to love them with Christ's love that flows in you.

Letting Go of Rejection Releases Your Supply

Friend, Jesus paid the price for you to walk free in forgiveness. He broke those chains of rejection that try to bind your soul. When you make a decision to walk in God's love, you can release those who've wounded you and give your heart freely to others.

Don't let unforgiveness poison your supply! Instead, choose to forgive others just as Christ has forgiven you. Take those hurts to the Lord, confess them, and let His healing power flood your soul. As you release God's love, you can freely give of your supply to others. If you do these things, unforgiveness won't stop you in your race, because there is nothing more powerful than the love of God!

STUDY QUESTIONS

> Be diligent to present yourself approved to God, a worker
> who does not need to be ashamed, rightly dividing the word of truth.
> — 2 Timothy 2:15

1. Considering what we have covered in this lesson, list some spiritual and physical consequences of holding on to unforgiveness and bitterness.

2. Hebrews 12:1 says, "Therefore we also, since we are surrounded by so great a cloud of witnesses, let us lay aside every weight, and the sin which so easily ensnares us, and let us run with endurance the race that is set before us." Now read Second Corinthias 11:24-28. After reading about Paul's experiences with rejection, what are some "weights" you think he may have had to lay aside as he ran his race?

PRACTICAL APPLICATION

> But be doers of the word,
> and not hearers only, deceiving yourselves.
> — James 1:22

1. Bitterness and rejection are powerful emotions that can imprison our heart, attitudes, thoughts, actions, and behaviors. Have you ever let unforgiveness or rejection hinder you from running your race? What were the consequences?

2. The love of God is greater than any hate, hurt, anger, or offense. It's more powerful than any assault or damage someone might have inflicted against you. What are some adjustments you can make in your life to allow God's love to flow freely from your heart to those around you — even to those who hurt you?

3. Hebrews 12:2 says, "Looking unto Jesus, the author and finisher of our faith, who for the joy that was set before Him endured the

cross…." Even though the people Jesus gave His life for had spit on, beaten, and rejected Him, Jesus was still able to ask the Father to forgive them. How does this impact your willingness to forgive others?

---

[1] "Forgiveness: Your Health Depends on It," Johns Hopkins Medicine, accessed October 22, 2024, https://www.hopkinsmedicine.org/health/wellness-and-prevention/forgiveness-your-health-depends-on-it.

LESSON 4

TOPIC
The Power of Forgiveness

SCRIPTURES

1. **Proverbs 4:23** — Keep your heart with all diligence, For out of it spring the issues of life.
2. **John 20:19-22** — Then, the same day at evening, being the first day of the week, when the doors were shut where the disciples were assembled, for fear of the Jews, Jesus came and stood in the midst, and said to them, "Peace be with you." When He had said this, He showed them His hands and His side. Then the disciples were glad when they saw the Lord. So Jesus said to them again, "Peace to you! As the Father has sent Me, I also send you." And when He had said this, He breathed on them, and said to them, "Receive the Holy Spirit."
3. **Acts 7:54-60** — When they heard these things they were cut to the heart, and they gnashed at him with their teeth. But he, being full of the Holy Spirit, gazed into heaven and saw the glory of God, and Jesus standing at the right hand of God, and said, "Look! I see the heavens opened and the Son of Man standing at the right hand of God!" Then they cried out with a loud voice, stopped their ears, and ran at him with one accord; and they cast him out of the city and stoned him. And the witnesses laid down their clothes at the feet of a young man named Saul. And they stoned Stephen as he was calling on God and saying, "Lord Jesus, receive my spirit." Then he knelt

down and cried out with a loud voice, "Lord, do not charge them with this sin." And when he had said this, he fell asleep.
4. **Luke 23:34** — Then Jesus said, "Father, forgive them, for they do not know what they do." And they divided His garments and cast lots.
5. **Matthew 18:23-35** — Therefore the kingdom of heaven is like a certain king who wanted to settle accounts with his servants. And when he had begun to settle accounts, one was brought to him who owed him ten thousand talents. But as he was not able to pay, his master commanded that he be sold, with his wife and children and all that he had, and that payment be made. The servant therefore fell down before him, saying, "Master, have patience with me, and I will pay you all." Then the master of that servant was moved with compassion, released him, and forgave him the debt. But that servant went out and found one of his fellow servants who owed him a hundred denarii; and he laid hands on him and took him by the throat, saying, "Pay me what you owe!" So his fellow servant fell down at his feet and begged him, saying, "Have patience with me, and I will pay you all." And he would not, but went and threw him into prison till he should pay the debt. So when his fellow servants saw what had been done, they were very grieved, and came and told their master all that had been done. Then his master, after he had called him, said to him, "You wicked servant! I forgave you all that debt because you begged me. Should you not also have had compassion on your fellow servant, just as I had pity on you?" And his master was angry, and delivered him to the torturers until he should pay all that was due him. "So My heavenly Father also will do to you if each of you, from his heart, does not forgive his brother his trespasses."

SYNOPSIS

God has a design, destiny, and purpose for your life, and He doesn't want *anything* to clog up the supply of the Spirit in you that helps you walk in that divine plan! By releasing others through forgiveness, you have an opportunity to walk in the light of Christ and to forgive others just as you have been forgiven by Him. In this lesson, Denise will dive deeper into the powerful effect forgiveness can have on your life.

The emphasis of this lesson:

Since unforgiveness is the devil's playground, it can open the door to sickness and disease in our lives. By taking the sting of offense to the Cross and allowing forgiveness to flow from our hearts, we remove many obstacles to our healing. As a result, we can enjoy a healthy soul and a healthy body just by walking in forgiveness. Furthermore, forgiveness releases others and cuts the string of offense tying us to that person. When we choose to follow Christ's example of forgiveness, we are exemplifying His great mercy toward those around us.

During our study, we have learned about the amazing power of being a "joint" in the Body of Christ, the danger of comparison, the importance of letting go of the past, and the power of releasing rejection and receiving the love of God instead. And renewing our mind to these things, we will become even more free to release the supply within us to those around us.

As we look at forgiveness and its power in our lives, we must understand that bottling up unforgiveness inside our hearts can poison our supply of the Spirit within us and hinder us from running our race. Unforgiveness is a powerful force the enemy uses to defeat so many Christians and keep them from accomplishing God's work in the earth. But by turning away from unforgiveness and turning toward forgiveness, we release God's supernatural power. As a result, any sickness that may have had us bound up can be miraculously healed.

Healing Through Forgiveness

What we allow to grow in our hearts affects our spiritual, physical, mental, and emotional health. Proverbs 4:23 instructs, "Keep your heart with all diligence, for out of it spring the issues of life." If unforgiveness manages to lodge itself deep in our hearts, it can poison the well of life flowing from inside us. Watching over our hearts is essential to both our present and our future!

In the last program, Denise shared her testimony of how her choice to let go of bitterness and unforgiveness made room for God's healing power to work in her body. For two years, Denise's hands and feet were unexplainably and painfully cold all the time. She was also tremendously fearful, and she experienced tormenting thoughts that resulted in panic attacks. But the Lord showed Denise that unforgiveness had taken root in her heart and was causing her to become sick.

One day the Holy Spirit spoke to Denise through a minister who knew nothing about what she'd been experiencing in her body and mind. He pointed to her and said, "You are a very sensitive person, and you have broken places on the inside of you. But you're going to wake up in a different world tomorrow morning."

When Denise went to bed that night, she was finally able to repent and release forgiveness to this person. The next morning, she woke up completely free! Her hands were no longer cold, the fear was gone, and the vice that had gripped her mind had been released. It was through the power of forgiveness that she became healed and whole.

Forgiveness is a choice, and we each have the ability to release forgiveness from our hearts toward others. The tentacles of unforgiveness and bitterness can wrap themselves around us, but if we'll choose to forgive others, the power of God can set us free!

Releasing Others Through Forgiveness

John 20:19-23 says:

> **Then, the same day at evening, being the first day of the week, when the doors were shut where the disciples were assembled, for fear of the Jews, Jesus came and stood in the midst, and said to them, 'Peace be with you.' When He had said this, He showed them His hands and His side. Then the disciples were glad when they saw the Lord. So Jesus said to them again, 'Peace to you! As the Father has sent Me, I also send you.' And when He had said this, He breathed on them, and said to them, 'Receive the Holy Spirit. If you forgive the sins of any, they are forgiven them; if you retain the sins of any, they are retained.'**

In verse 22, Jesus breathed on the disciples, and it was at that very moment that the Holy Spirit came to live on the inside of them — they were born again. It's interesting to note that the first thing Jesus taught the freshly born-again disciples was the power of forgiveness. He said, "If you forgive the sins of any, they are forgiven them; if you retain the sins of any, they are retained."

With the new birth, the disciples were equipped to forgive others with the love of God. That same truth still applies to us today. Because of the new life of Christ on the inside of us, we are equipped with God's power to release love and forgiveness to others.

Unforgiveness is like a thread — it keeps us connected to the one who offended us. But when we choose to forgive, that string is cut, and that offense no longer has power over us. In fact, forgiveness can begin a brand-new cycle of life and healing!

A powerful example of releasing someone through forgiveness is found during the stoning of Stephen:

> **When they heard these things they were cut to the heart, and they gnashed at him with their teeth. But he, being full of the Holy Spirit, gazed into heaven and saw the glory of God, and Jesus standing at the right hand of God, and said, 'Look! I see the heavens opened and the Son of Man standing at the right hand of God!' Then they cried out with a loud voice, stopped their ears, and ran at him with one accord; and they cast him out of the city and stoned him. And the witnesses laid down their clothes at the feet of a young man named Saul. And they stoned Stephen as he was calling on God and saying, 'Lord Jesus, receive my spirit.' Then he knelt down and cried out with a loud voice, 'Lord, do not charge them with this sin.' And when he had said this, he fell asleep.**
>
> — Acts 7:54-60

In most places in Scripture, Jesus is described as being seated at the right hand of God. But when Stephen, the very first martyr, was just about to be stoned for preaching the Gospel, he looked up and saw Jesus *standing* at the right hand of God. Seeing Jesus in that way encouraged Stephen so much that he told everyone what he was seeing.

His executioners then took Stephen out of the city and, according to what history tells us, they put him in a deep hole to stone him. They heaved huge stones at him in an attempt to break his skull, crush his bones, and, eventually, end his life. While all of that was happening, Stephen prepared to die and said, "Lord Jesus, receive my spirit."

Then with seconds of breath left in Stephen's lungs, he knelt down and cried out, "Lord, do not charge them with this sin." In his most painful moment, Stephen chose to forgive those who were attacking him. When he spoke those words, he was setting free every man and woman who was participating in his execution — including the young man named Saul, who was holding the clothes of those who were stoning Stephen. That young man grew up to become the apostle Paul who wrote the vast majority of the New Testament!

Stephen didn't know the impact Saul would later have on the world for thousands of years to come. He was simply allowing the love of God to flow through him and choosing to forgive the people who were committing a horrendous evil against him. As a result, the whole Church was impacted dramatically and two-thirds of the New Covenant — the divinely inspired Word of God — was brought into the world.

The Most Powerful Example of Forgiveness

Jesus provided the most significant example of forgiveness when He forgave his crucifiers. As blood was pouring down His wounded body, He looked on those who were beating, mocking, and cursing Him and had compassion on them. He said, "...Father, forgive them, for they do not know what they do..." (Luke 23:34). His act of forgiveness was the greatest display of love in the history of the world, and it had eternal effects on all of humanity — past, present, and future!

Because of Jesus' great love toward us, we can forgive others even when they've hurt us, lied about us, betrayed us, or stolen from us. Perhaps they didn't understand what they were doing or didn't know how badly their actions hurt us. But when we choose to forgive, we release them from that offense and set them free.

We are hindered in our own journey through life when we don't forgive. But many times, the people who have hurt us are hindered in their journey as well. When we extend forgiveness to those who have wronged us and release them of all guilt, they are given the opportunity to move forward in their own journey without the weight of their mistakes.

Jesus said, "If you forgive the sins of any, they are forgiven them; if you retain the sins of any, they are retained" (John 20:23). When we forgive, we not only keep our own heart right and walk in the freedom Christ purchased for us, but we also help others walk free of the shame that hangs over their heads and consumes their minds and emotions over of what they've done. When we walk in love and forgive others, we not only free ourselves to fulfill God's plan for our life, but we also release those who have wronged us so they can fulfill the amazing plans God has for their lives too. After all, this is what Jesus did for us!

While Jesus was dying on the Cross, he said, "…Father, forgive them, for they do not know what they do…" (Luke 23:34). If you had been present at Jesus' crucifixion, it would have been difficult to believe that the soldiers who beat Jesus beyond recognition, hammered the nails into His hands and feet, and pierced His side didn't know what they were doing. But Jesus looked on them and had compassion, saying, "They know not what they do." He saw beyond the rejection and betrayal and chose to forgive.

You may be thinking, *You don't know what happened to me; they knew exactly what they were doing.* But Jesus is calling you and the rest of His Body to a higher way. The Bible says that those who wrong you don't know what they are doing, and Jesus is asking you to forgive accordingly — for your sake and theirs.

The Merciful Master

Another great example of releasing others through forgiveness is found in a parable Jesus shared in Matthew 18:23-27:

> **Therefore the kingdom of heaven is like a certain king who wanted to settle accounts with his servants. And when he had begun to settle accounts, one was brought to him who owed him ten thousand talents. But as he was not able to pay, his master commanded that he be sold, with his wife and children and all that he had, and that payment be made. The servant therefore fell down before him, saying, 'Master, have patience with me, and I will pay you all.' Then the master of that servant was moved with compassion, released him, and forgave him the debt.**

When confronted about the debt he owed, the servant pleaded with his master to have mercy on him and patiently wait for him to pay the debt in full. But the master, filled with compassion, forgave him for his delinquency and let him go free.

Just like the master in this parable, Jesus has forgiven us our debt of sin. No matter how good we are or how many good deeds we do, we will never be able to come up with enough to pay our debt. But because of Jesus' blood, we can walk away from the payment of sin completely free! He took our place and has released us from the debt we couldn't pay.

But the parable Jesus told in Matthew 18 continues in verses 28-30:

> **But that servant went out and found one of his fellow servants who owed him a hundred denarii; and he laid hands on him and took him by the throat, saying, 'Pay me what you owe!' So his fellow servant fell down at his feet and begged him, saying, 'Have patience with me, and I will pay you all.' And he would not, but went and threw him into prison till he should pay the debt.**

The very same servant who had experienced such great mercy from his master didn't demonstrate that tenderness to others in his life. He went out to find his fellow servant who owed him money and demanded repayment immediately — a debt that was equivalent to only about 20 U.S. dollars by today's standards. Instead of freely showing mercy to his fellow man, the servant withheld forgiveness and sent his fellow servant to prison until he was able to pay off the debt.

This was not at all the response the merciful master wanted his servant to have toward his fellow man. And because of this servant's lack of compassion, a grave consequence followed (*see* Matthew 18:31-35).

Forgive and You Will Be Forgiven

The Father has forgiven us a huge debt, and because of that, He asks us to forgive others. Jesus even includes this principle of forgiveness in the Lord's Prayer found in Matthew 6:9-13 when He tells us how to pray. Verse 12 says, "And forgive us our debts, as we forgive our debtors."

Sadly, many Christians turn around and refuse to forgive others for the wrongs they have done to them. Although they have received mercy from God, they won't extend to others that same compassion and kindness that God bestowed to them. This is not the way Christ taught us to live.

God wants more for us than simply our enjoying the freedom of forgiveness and the joy of having Heaven in our future. He wants us to allow the love that has been shed abroad in our hearts by the Holy Ghost to shine through us and set others free of the guilt and shame that comes with sin.

Friend, you have a choice today to release others through forgiveness. You don't have to be like that unfaithful servant who chose not to forgive when he himself was forgiven. Rather, you can look to Jesus — the Author and Finisher of your faith — and receive His power to forgive all those who have hurt you, taken from you, talked bad about you, or done you wrong. Just like Stephen who released others even at his death, you, too, can follow in Jesus' footsteps and forgive your enemies. The life of God dwells on the inside of you — and you have the ability to give from what you've been given in Christ. You can live in the freedom of forgiveness today!

STUDY QUESTIONS

> Be diligent to present yourself approved to God, a worker
> who does not need to be ashamed, rightly dividing the word of truth.
> — 2 Timothy 2:15

1. Read Acts 7:54-60. The Bible doesn't give details about Stephen's internal experience during his stoning, but when he looked up to Heaven, what Stephen saw had an impact on his response to his murderers. Considering Stephen's recorded words and actions, take a few minutes to imagine what may have been going through Stephen's heart and mind during his final moments.

2. When we forgive others, we keep our own heart right, making it possible for us to walk in the freedom Christ purchased for us. What impact does our choice to forgive others have on those who have wronged us?

3. Read Matthew 18:31-34. What happened to the man who would not forgive his fellow servant? Why do you think there was a consequence for his actions?

PRACTICAL APPLICATION

> But be doers of the word,
> and not hearers only, deceiving yourselves.
> — James 1:22

1. Proverbs 4:23 instructs, "Keep your heart with all diligence, for out of it spring the issues of life." What are some steps you can take to safeguard your heart against harboring unforgiveness?

2. Think of a time when it was difficult for you to forgive someone who wronged you. Have you forgiven that person? Have you allowed unforgiveness to linger in your heart? If you have forgiven that person, describe how you were able to do it. If you have not forgiven that person, take a few moments to pray and ask the Holy Spirit to help you allow His love to flow through you toward him or her.
3. No matter how good we are or how many good deeds we do, we will never be able to pay our debt of sin. But because of Jesus' blood, we can walk in complete freedom. How does this truth affect your willingness to extend forgiveness to those who have hurt you?

LESSON 5

TOPIC
Turning Away From Negative Opinions

SCRIPTURES
1. **John 7:3-5** — His brothers therefore said to Him, 'Depart from here and go into Judea, that Your disciples also may see the works that You are doing. For no one does anything in secret while he himself seeks to be known openly. If You do these things, show Yourself to the world.' For even His brothers did not believe Him.
2. **John 7:12** — And there was much complaining among the people concerning Him. Some said, 'He is good'; others said, 'No, on the contrary, He deceives the people.'
3. **John 7:15** — And the Jews marveled, saying, 'How does this Man know letters, having never studied?'
4. **John 7:20** — The people answered and said, 'you have a demon. Who is seeking to kill You?'
5. **John 7:31** — And many of the people believed in Him, and said, 'When the Christ comes, will He do more signs than these which this Man has done?'
6. **John 7:41** — Others said, 'This is the Christ.' But some said, 'Will the Christ come out of Galilee?'

7. **John 7:46** — The officers answered, 'No man ever spoke like this Man!'
8. **John 7:53** — And everyone went to his own house.
9. **John 8:1-10** — But Jesus went to the Mount of Olives. Now early in the morning He came again into the temple, and all the people came to Him; and He sat down and taught them. Then the scribes and Pharisees brought to Him a woman caught in adultery. And when they had set her in the mist, they said to Him, 'Teacher, this woman was caught in adultery, in the very act. Now Moses, in the law, commanded us that such should be stoned. But what do You say?' This they said, testing Him, that they might have something of which to accuse Him. But Jesus stooped down and wrote on the ground with His finger, as though He did not hear. So when they continued asking Him, He raised Himself up and said to them, 'He who is without sin among you, let him throw a stone at her first.' And again He stooped down and wrote on the ground. Then those who heard it, being convicted by their conscience, went out one by one, beginning with the oldest even to the last. And Jesus was left alone, and the woman standing in the midst. When Jesus had raised Himself up and saw no one but the woman, He said to her, 'Woman, where are those accusers of yours? Has no one condemned you?'

SYNOPSIS

God's thoughts and opinions of you carry more weight than anyone else's. You must refuse to be influenced by the negative opinions of others — or the negative thoughts you may have about yourself — and stay focused on what God says about you. The enemy will use things like offense, the fear of man, and the opinions of others in an attempt to stop you from fulfilling God's plan and giving the supply of the Spirit within you. But when you prioritize God's opinion, you can press forward in His plan regardless of whether people praise you or criticize you. His opinion is the only one that matters!

The emphasis of this lesson:

Being persuaded by the opinions of others can cause us to waver in our direction and lose focus on what God has really called us to do. If we live for the praise of men or become despondent by the opinions of others, we'll never accomplish our assignment. Thankfully, we can follow Jesus' example and respond with kindness, wisdom, and quietness when

barraged by contradictory opinions. When we understand that God's opinion is the only one that counts, we will no longer be chained to the cycle of living to please men. Instead, we'll be free to live for God, please Him in all we do, and give from our supply!

There are many things that can block the supply of the Holy Spirit from flowing freely through us and touching the world around us. In the first lessons of our study, we learned about the amazing power of being a "joint" in the Body of Christ, the danger of comparison, the importance of letting go of the past, and the powerful force of forgiveness that sets us and those who have wronged us free.

In this lesson, we will see how Jesus responded to the gossip of the general public, the deceitful questions of religious leaders and cultural authority figures of that time, and the lack of belief from even His closest family members. Let's dive in and learn how Jesus allowed the supply of the Spirit in Him to not only help Him fulfill His purpose, but to set a sinful woman on a path of freedom and righteousness.

Unbelief, Gossip, and Varying Opinions

Did you know seeking the approval of others can hinder you in your race? If you place too much value on what other people think of you and what you're doing, you can easily become distracted by all those voices talking to you! If you want to run your race well and remain unstoppable all the way to the end, you must take heed in how you respond to the opinions of others.

There will always be people who have negative opinions and oppose us. There will always be people who dislike us. There will always be people who oppose the Gospel. But none of that kept Jesus from fulfilling His purpose, and it shouldn't stop us either! Let's take a closer look at how Jesus responded to the opinions of others.

In John 7, we see that there was a plethora of opinions surrounding Jesus and His ministry. When Jesus came to Galilee, his own brothers expressed their opinions of how and when His ministry should be seen publicly.

> His brothers therefore said to Him, 'Depart from here and go into Judea, that Your disciples also may see the works that You are doing. For no one does anything in secret while he himself

seeks to be known openly. If You do these things, show Yourself to the world.' For even His brothers did not believe in Him.
— **John 7:3,4**

Jesus' *own family* didn't believe in Him! They accused Him of merely wanting to be famous, they pressured Him to dismiss God's plan, and they put Him down. But instead of getting upset or argumentative, Jesus kept moving forward with God's plan. Jesus knew in his heart what the Father was leading Him to do, and He wasn't going to allow His earthly brothers to talk Him out of His obedient surrender to the timing of God. It's so important that we do the same thing and move forward in life with what's inside of us — what God has said to us and what He says about us.

Jesus was tempted just like we are, yet He was without sin (*see* Hebrews 4:15). He understands the pressure of trying to stick to God's plan in spite of others' opinions. He understands the power that others' opinions can lord over us. But Jesus overcame those temptations so that He could make a way for us to overcome. Jesus held God's opinion above everyone else's, and in turn, He fulfilled God's divine plan for His life!

Let's take a look at John 7 and see some of the varying opinions people had about Jesus:

- **Verse 12** — "And there was much complaining among the people concerning Him. Some said, 'He is good'; others said, 'No, on the contrary, He deceives the people.'"
- **Verse 15** — "And the Jews marveled, saying, 'How does this Man know letters, having never studied?'"
- **Verse 20** — "The people answered and said, 'You have a demon. Who is seeking to kill You?'"
- **Verse 31** — "And many of the people believed in Him, and said, 'When the Christ comes, will He do more signs than these which this Man has done?'"
- **Verse 40,41** — "Therefore many from the crowd, when they heard this saying, said, 'Truly this is the Prophet.' Others said, 'This is the Christ....'"
- **Verse 46** — "The officers answered, 'No man ever spoke like this Man!'"

Jesus was surrounded by people who believed in Him and others who did not approve of Him. But He didn't wait for their approval or praise before He did what God had sent Him to do. And He didn't allow negative opinions or gossip to stop Him from obeying God. He was confident in what God had placed in Him.

In each of the cases mentioned in John 7, Jesus' response was to simply continue on with His ministry as the Father led Him. He wasn't influenced one way or another by the praise or the criticism of men. Jesus remained focused on what He heard the Father say and didn't let the negative opinions of others affect Him — and that is what we must do. We must move forward according to the conviction we have in our heart rather than according to the approval or negative opinions of others.

If we are ruled by the opinions of others, then we are allowing those people to define our identity. And if we are not careful, we will find ourselves being manipulated and moved along in life instead of being led by the Spirit of God and the convictions in our heart. But the bottom line is, we will have to stand before God in the end, not those people. We must live to please God above all else.

Jesus Sought the Heart of God

After everyone expressed their opinions of Jesus, the people simply went home (*see* John 7:53). But Jesus went somewhere else. John 8:1 says, "But Jesus went to the Mount of Olives." The Mount of Olives is where Jesus often went to pray and fellowship with God.

After hearing all that the people had to say, Jesus went to pray and seek the heart of the Father. He retreated to His quiet place and didn't let the opinions of others weigh Him down. Instead, He spent time being refreshed by God.

When Jesus returned to the Temple on the next day, something unusual took place. We read about it in John 8:2-5:

> **Now early in the morning He came again into the temple, and all the people came to Him; and He sat down and taught them. Then the scribes and Pharisees brought to Him a woman caught in adultery. And when they had set her in the midst, they said to Him, 'Teacher, this woman was caught in adultery, in**

the very act. Now Moses, in the law, commanded us that such should be stoned. But what do You say?'

The religious leaders brought before Jesus a woman who had been caught in adultery. The Greek text indicates that they didn't merely ask Jesus one time, "What do You say?" No, they began to hammer, badger, and question Him about the proper way to handle her sin.

Jesus' response to the religious leaders' attempts to catch Him saying something wrong is recorded in verse six, which says, "This they said, testing Him, that they might have something of which to accuse Him. But Jesus stooped down and wrote on the ground with His finger, as though He did not hear." The Bible doesn't tell us what He wrote on the ground, but we do know what He said next. What happened was amazing:

> **So when they continued asking Him, He raised Himself up and said to them, 'He who is without sin among you, let him throw a stone at her first.' And again He stooped down and wrote on the ground. Then those who heard it, being convicted by their conscience, went out one by one, beginning with the oldest even to the last. And Jesus was left alone, and the woman standing in the midst.**
> —John 8:7-9

Jesus was in an extremely difficult position because of the nature of the question the Pharisees were asking Him. The Roman law said that the woman who had been caught in the act of adultery was deserving of capital punishment for her actions, and the Jewish law agreed that she should be stoned. The Pharisees had come up with a question that they thought would cause Jesus to break the law no matter what He said and therefore discredit Himself.

The scheming religious leaders had taken advantage of this woman's sinful circumstances and set out to condemn and trap Jesus. He was in a seemingly impossible situation with His reputation on the line, and a desperate woman's life depended on the answer He would give.

This was a woman who had been caught in the *very act* of sexual sin and stood rightfully accused by both the Roman and Jewish laws. But in that moment, Jesus chose to seek the opinion of His Father. The Father's heart was full of compassion for this woman. God's opinion was to extend love and restoration to her, not judgment or even dismissal.

There may be times when it is tempting to ignore a difficult situation or dismiss someone who is in trouble. But the power of God is inside us. We can slow down and seek God's thoughts and opinion about a situation and act according to what *He* says. The supply of the Spirit inside us gives us access to God's heart and empowers us to walk in wisdom, boldness, love, and compassion in every situation.

The Most Important Opinion

John 8:10-12 gives us a glimpse into the heart and mind of God by telling us how Jesus treated the woman.

> **When Jesus had raised Himself up and saw no one but the woman, He said to her, 'Woman, where are those accusers of yours? Has no one condemned you?' She said, 'No one, Lord.' And Jesus said to her, 'Neither do I condemn you; go and sin no more.'**

The woman didn't argue with Jesus and say things like, "You don't know how bad I am; I deserve the punishment." No, she simply received what Jesus said and accepted His opinion of her above the others. We can learn from this woman! Regardless of what she had done, and regardless of the opinions of others, she chose to esteem Jesus' opinion and what He said about her.

Whether someone's opinion of you is positive or negative, if it doesn't line up with what God has spoken about you, do not allow it to define you. When you are surrounded by the clamoring voices of others, take a moment to remember how Jesus responded to the opinions of men.

No matter what others said or thought about Him, Jesus remained focused on His mission and His identity as the Son of God. When Jesus was faced with varying opinions from those around Him, He was patient and kind. He didn't strike back, become argumentative, or lose His temper. Jesus simply dismissed all those opinions, because His value and His assignment weren't hinging on what people thought of Him.

Instead of waiting on the approval of others, keep your eyes on Jesus and what He has commissioned you to do. You must keep moving forward in your assignment according to the conviction in your own heart. And remember, your Heavenly Father is so brilliant! He can give you the answer you need for any problem. Even when man tries to ensnare you,

He will give you the wisdom to handle tricky situations just as Jesus did. When you spend time alone in prayer with the Father, you are well prepared to navigate any difficulty with the wisdom of God.

There is only one opinion God expects you to live by — and that is His opinion of who you are and what His plan is for your life. When you're tempted to change your direction just because someone praises or criticizes you, take a step back from the situation and refocus. By staying focused on His opinion, you can remain unstoppable in this life and allow the supply of the Holy Spirit in you to flow freely!

STUDY QUESTIONS

> Be diligent to present yourself approved to God, a worker who does not need to be ashamed, rightly dividing the word of truth.
> — 2 Timothy 2:15

1. John 7:3 and 4 records the opinions Jesus' brothers had about Him. What thoughts and feelings do you think Jesus might have had to overcome after receiving criticism from His own family?
2. John 8:1 says, "But Jesus went to the Mount of Olives." After hearing all the varying opinions of the general public, Jesus left to pray and seek the heart of His Father. How did this response prepare Jesus for His coming interaction with the Pharisees and the woman caught in adultery?
3. Read John 8:2-8. Jesus was in an extremely difficult position because of the nature of the question the Pharisees were asking Him, and a desperate woman's life was on the line. Why do you think Jesus stopped to write on the ground? What do you think He was doing?

PRACTICAL APPLICATION

> But be doers of the word, and not hearers only, deceiving yourselves.
> — James 1:22

1. John 7:6-9 says, "Then Jesus said to them, 'My time has not yet come.... You go up to this feast. I am not yet going up to this feast, for My time has not yet fully come.' When He had said these things to them, He remained in Galilee." Describe a time when you

decided to obey God regardless of what others thought you should do. What were the consequences of your decision?

2. Read Luke 21:37 and 22:39. Jesus was accustomed to going to the Mount of Olives to pray — especially when He was faced with difficult situations. However, when Jesus was confronted by the Pharisees in John 8, He wasn't able to retreat to the Mount of Olives to pray. He simply stopped and prayed in the moment. How often do you seek the heart of God *in the moment* when you are faced with difficult situations?

3. No matter what others said or thought about Him, Jesus always remained focused on His mission and His identity as the Son of God. Take a few moments to search for and write out at least one Bible verse that testifies of God's opinion about you. It may be regarding your life's calling or even about what Jesus has done for you through redemption. Make the decision now to place God's opinion above all others and be prepared to respond with His Word any time you are faced with a contrary opinion.

LESSON 6

TOPIC
Victory in Agreeing With God

SCRIPTURES

1. **Daniel 3:13-29** — Then Nebuchadnezzar, in rage and fury, gave the command to bring Shadrach, Meshach, and Abed-Nego. So they brought these men before the king. Nebuchadnezzar spoke, saying to them, "Is it true, Shadrach, Meshach, and Abed-Nego, that you do not serve my gods or worship the gold image which I have set up? Now if you are ready at the time you hear the sound of the horn, flute, harp, lyre, and psaltery, in symphony with all kinds of music, and you fall down and worship the image which I have made, good! But if you do not worship, you shall be cast immediately into the midst of a burning fiery furnace. And who is the god who will deliver you from my hands?" Shadrach, Meshach, and Abed-Nego answered and said to the king, "O Nebuchadnezzar, we have no need to

answer you in this matter. If that is the case, our God whom we serve is able to deliver us from the burning fiery furnace, and He will deliver us from your hand, O king. But if not, let it be known to you, O king, that we do not serve your gods, nor will we worship the gold image which you have set up." Then Nebuchadnezzar was full of fury, and the expression on his face changed toward Shadrach, Meshach, and Abed-Nego. He spoke and commanded that they heat the furnace seven times more than it was usually heated. And he commanded certain mighty men of valor who were in his army to bind Shadrach, Meshach, and Abed-Nego, and cast them into the burning fiery furnace. Then these men were bound in their coats, their trousers, their turbans, and their other garments, and were cast into the midst of the burning fiery furnace. Therefore, because the king's command was urgent, and the furnace exceedingly hot, the flame of the fire killed those men who took up Shadrach, Meshach, and Abed-Nego. And these three men, Shadrach, Meshach, and Abed-Nego, fell down bound into the midst of the burning fiery furnace. Then King Nebuchadnezzar was astonished; and he rose in haste and spoke, saying to his counselors, "Did we not cast three men bound into the midst of the fire?" They answered and said to the king, "True, O king." "Look!" he answered, "I see four men loose, walking in the midst of the fire; and they are not hurt, and the form of the fourth is like the Son of God." Then Nebuchadnezzar went near the mouth of the burning fiery furnace and spoke, saying, "Shadrach, Meshach, and Abed-Nego, servants of the Most High God, come out, and come here." Then Shadrach, Meshach, and Abed-Nego came from the midst of the fire. And the satraps, administrators, governors, and the king's counselors gathered together, and they saw these men on whose bodies the fire had no power; the hair of their head was not singed nor were their garments affected, and the smell of fire was not on them. Nebuchadnezzar spoke, saying, "Blessed be the God of Shadrach, Meshach, and Abed-Nego, who sent His Ange and delivered His servants who trusted in Him, and they have frustrated the king's word, and yielded their bodies, that they should not serve nor worship any god except their own God! Therefore I make a decree that any people, nation, or language which speaks anything amiss against the God of Shadrach, Meshach, and Abed-Nego shall be cut in pieces, and their houses shall be made an ash heap; because there is no other God who can deliver like this."

SYNOPSIS

Standing for God is not always easy, but you never have to do it alone. The unstoppable power of the Holy Spirit in you is always present — especially when you take a stand against the enemy. The Holy Spirit, who is just like Jesus, lives inside you and empowers you to stand firmly on the Word of God no matter the circumstances. Even if no one else stands with you, the Most High God is on your side, and He will deliver you!

The emphasis of this lesson:

Shadrach, Meshach, and Abednego were three young Hebrew men who were faced with a choice to either obey God's Word or bow to the demands of a wicked king. When they refused to worship anyone besides *their* God, the king was not happy, but God came to their defense!

In previous lessons, we have learned about God's unstoppable power within us that makes us each a "joint" in the Body of Christ. We've also looked at the danger of comparison, the importance of letting go of the past, the power of forgiveness, and how to avoid letting the opinions of others stop us from fulfilling our purpose.

In this lesson, we will be diving into the well-known Old Testament story of how King Nebuchadnezzar commissioned a golden statue of himself to be built and then commanded the people to bow before it. Among the people were three very bold Hebrew children who refused to bow to the golden image of the king. In a sea of thousands of bowing subjects, Shadrach, Meshach, and Abednego stood their ground. Our story for this lesson begins with the king's response to their defiance, recorded in Daniel 3:13.

The Fury of the King

> **Then Nebuchadnezzar, in rage and fury, gave the command to bring Shadrach, Meshach, and Abed-Nego. So they brought these men before the king.**
> — Daniel 3:13

Shadrach, Meshach, and Abednego were Hebrews living in the foreign land of Babylon, so these were not their original names. Being Hebrew, these young men would have been taught from an early age about God and His laws, and, as you'll soon see, their identities were found in Him.

The names Shadrach, Meshach, and Abednego had meanings that were contrary to what they knew to be the truth and that gave praise to false gods. By giving the Hebrew children these new names, the Babylonian culture was essentially saying, "You are not who you think you are," and, "We are giving you a new label and changing your identity." This is the level of power King Nebuchadnezzar was able to exercise over the Hebrew people who lived in Babylon. Can you imagine the pressure these three young men must have been under?

But Shadrach, Meshach, and Abednego were so strongly convicted by what they knew about their God that they refused to bow to the golden statue of the king. The king's command is found in Daniel 3:14 and 15:

> **Nebuchadnezzar spoke, saying to them, "Is it true, Shadrach, Meshach, and Abed-Nego, that you do not serve my gods or worship the gold image which I have set up? Now if you are ready at the time you hear the sound of the horn, flute, harp, lyre, and psaltery, in symphony with all kinds of music, and you fall down and worship the image which I have made, good! But if you do not worship, you shall be cast immediately into the midst of a burning fiery furnace. And who is the god who will deliver you from my hands?"**

Does the king's threat sound familiar? Nebuchadnezzar arrogantly tried to coerce and terrorize the three men, saying, "...If you do not worship, you shall be cast immediately into the midst of a burning fiery furnace. And who is the god who will deliver you from my hands?"

That sounds just like the devil when he begins to stir up problems in our lives! The enemy has no new tricks. When we are faced with difficult circumstances — sickness, relationship problems, or even financial issues — we are also confronted with the enemy's threats that say things like, *Who will deliver you from my hands?*

But we can learn something important from the way Shadrach, Meshach, and Abednego responded to the king's threats. The story continues in Daniel 3:16 and 17:

> **Shadrach, Meshach, and Abed-Nego answered and said to the king, "O Nebuchadnezzar, we have no need to answer you in this matter. If that is the case, our God whom we serve is able to**

deliver us from the burning fiery furnace, and He will deliver us from your hand, O king.

'He Is *My* God!'

The three young men essentially said, "Are you kidding? We will not bow to your false gods or to your image! Our God will deliver us." Don't you love how they called Him "our God"? Even though Jesus hadn't come, and the Holy Spirit hadn't yet been poured out, Shadrach, Meshach, and Abednego had a relationship with God. They knew something that we also need to know: When we face difficulties, trials, and the negative opinions of other people, we are not alone. He is *our* God even in the middle of trying situations!

Shadrach, Meshach, and Abednego knew God was *their* God. It's powerful to know whom you serve. You can stand up to your situation and say, "He's *my* God; He's *my* Deliverer!" Just like those three young Hebrew men said in Daniel 3:17, we can also say, "My God, whom I serve, is able to deliver me." Isn't it wonderful to know that even though you aren't perfect, you can still have confidence that *your* God will come through for you — no matter the circumstances?

But sometimes our circumstances "speak" to us, saying we'll never overcome, or we'll always have to deal with a particular problem. In that case, we must speak back to our circumstances! When the devil presents us with thoughts that are contrary to God's Word, we have the choice to accept or reject those thoughts.

In Daniel 3:18, we see that Shadrach, Meshach, and Abednego courageously said this to the king: "…Let it be known to you, O king, that we do not serve your gods, nor will we worship the gold image which you have set up." In response to the lying voice of the enemy, we must also say, "Let it be known, devil, I will not bow to you."

Nebuchadnezzar's furious response to Shadrach, Meshach, and Abednego's boldness is recorded in verses 19-22:

> **Then Nebuchadnezzar was full of fury, and the expression on his face changed toward Shadrach, Meshach, and Abed-Nego. He spoke and commanded that they heat the furnace seven times more than it was usually heated. And he commanded certain mighty men of valor who were in his army to bind**

> Shadrach, Meshach, and Abed-Nego, and cast them into the burning fiery furnace. Then these men were bound in their coats, their trousers, their turbans, and their other garments, and were cast into the midst of the burning fiery furnace. Therefore, because the king's command was urgent, and the furnace exceedingly hot, the flame of the fire killed those men who took up Shadrach, Meshach, and Abed-Nego.

The three young Hebrew men were faced with an impossible situation as they were cast into that burning fiery furnace, yet they stood their ground with boldness. They knew their God would rescue them one way or another. You can access that same boldness that was in Shadrach, Meshach, and Abednego because the same God who delivered them lives in you. That same unstoppable, unshakable, power of God is *in you*!

You don't have to bow to sickness or lack. You don't have to bow to the opinions of others or the negative opinions you may have of yourself. Your situation may *look* fiery and impossible, but you can stand up to the attacks of the enemy and boldly proclaim, "I will not bow to you!"

The Fourth Man in the Fire

Let's read in verses 23-28 what miraculously happened next to Shadrach, Meshach, and Abednego.

> And these three men, Shadrach, Meshach, and Abed-Nego, fell down bound into the midst of the burning fiery furnace. Then King Nebuchadnezzar was astonished; and he rose in haste and spoke, saying to his counselors, 'Did we not cast three men bound into the midst of the fire?' They answered and said to the king, 'True, O king.' 'Look!' he answered, 'I see four men loose, walking in the midst of the fire; and they are not hurt, and the form of the fourth is like the Son of God.'
> — Daniel 3:23-28

Wow! What a miracle! King Nebuchadnezzar was, at the time, the most powerful man in the world. He had commanded the executions of these three Hebrew men, and he expected to see his powerful command carried out. He expected to see them burning in the flames, disintegrating in the heat. But when the king looked into the furnace to witness this outcome, he not only saw the three men walking around freely in the flames, but there was a *fourth* man in the fire with them!

Friend, when you resist the devil and stand your ground according to what the Word of God says, the Greater One who lives in you is greater than the devil in this world, and He stands with you (*see* 1 John 4:4). When you refuse to bow to the attacks of the devil, no weapon formed against you will prosper (*see* Isaiah 54:17). As you make that stand and agree with the power of God and His promises, just like Shadrach, Meshach, and Abednego, you will not stand alone! The Holy Spirit on the inside of you who is just like Jesus also stands up alongside you and defends you. Hebrews 13:5 and 6 says, "…For He Himself has said, 'I will never leave you nor forsake you.' So we may boldly say: 'The Lord is my helper; I will not fear. What can man do to me?'" When we say no to the power of darkness, we invite the power of God to join in with us.

God's Power Will Amaze Others

Shadrach, Meshach, and Abednego's story continues in Daniel 3:26 and 27:

> **Then Nebuchadnezzar went near the mouth of the burning fiery furnace and spoke, saying, 'Shadrach, Meshach, and Abed-Nego, servants of the Most High God, come out, and come here.' Then Shadrach, Meshach, and Abed-Nego came from the midst of the fire. And the satraps, administrators, governors, and the king's counselors gathered together, and they saw these men on whose bodies the fire had no power; the hair of their head was not singed nor were their garments affected, and the smell of fire was not on them.**

When you stand for what is right, and when you humble yourself before God, He exalts you (*see* 1 Peter 5:6). When you stand up for God, you don't stand alone; He stands with you every time. He will always carry you through any difficult situation, and those around you will be amazed at the power of God at work on your behalf.

The men who had set the trap for Shadrach, Meshach, and Abednego — expecting them to be put to death — must have stood amazed as the power of God was manifested right before their eyes. And the king himself saw the fourth man in the fire with the young Hebrew men and was greatly impacted by the miracle he witnessed.

> **Nebuchadnezzar spoke, saying, 'Blessed be the God of Shadrach, Meshach, and Abed-Nego, who sent His Angel and delivered His servants who trusted in Him, and they have**

frustrated the king's word, and yielded their bodies, that they should not serve nor worship any god except their own God! Therefore I make a decree that any people, nation, or language which speaks anything amiss against the God of Shadrach, Meshach, and Abed-Nego shall be cut in pieces, and their houses shall be made an ash heap; because there is no other God who can deliver like this.'
— Daniel 3:28,29

When Shadrach, Meshach, and Abednego stood up for what they believed, not only did they make a way to experience the power of God for themselves, but they made a way for the most powerful man in the world, as well as the entire nation, to see God perform an incredible miracle. Don't underestimate the power you have inside you to influence and impact the lives of others. When you stand up for God, you stand up with the Holy Spirit, and He gives you the power to be *unstoppable*.

STUDY QUESTIONS

Be diligent to present yourself approved to God, a worker who does not need to be ashamed, rightly dividing the word of truth.
— 2 Timothy 2:15

1. What message was King Nebuchadnezzar sending by renaming the Hebrew children with Babylonian names that honored false gods?
2. How did Shadrach, Meshach, and Abednego's understanding of God shape their response to King Nebuchadnezzar's command?
3. Read Daniel 3:28 and 29. In what ways did the boldness of Shadrach, Meshach, and Abednego impact King Nebuchadnezzar, and what effect did it have on the culture of Babylon?

PRACTICAL APPLICATION

But be doers of the word, and not hearers only, deceiving yourselves.
— James 1:22

1. Have you ever had to stand up for your faith when everyone around you bowed to the demands of a wicked cultural expectation? Describe

your experience and note the impact your actions had on the people around you.
2. Shadrach, Meshach, and Abednego survived the fiery furnace, and, furthermore, they did not even smell like fire! How does knowing the Holy Spirit is with you change the way you approach difficult or seemingly impossible situations?
3. Make a list of five scriptures that declare your identity in Christ, and remind yourself of these truths by speaking them out loud every day this week. The next time you are faced with lies from the enemy about yourself or your situation, allow these verses to remind you that you are never alone in your stand of faith.

LESSON 7

TOPIC
Getting Past the Voices of Others

SCRIPTURES
1. **2 Corinthians 4:7** — But we have this treasure in earthen vessels, that the excellence of the power may be of God and not of us.
2. **1 Samuel 17:26-37** — Then David spoke to the men who stood by him, saying, "What shall be done for the man who kills this Philistine and takes away the reproach from Israel? For who is this uncircumcised Philistine, that he should defy the armies of the living God?" And the people answered him in this manner, saying, "So shall it be done for the man who kills him." Now Eliab his oldest brother heard when he spoke to the men; and Eliab's anger was aroused against David, and he said, "Why did you come down here? And with whom have you left those few sheep in the wilderness? I know your pride and the insolence of your heart, for you have come down to see the battle." And David said, "What have I done now? Is there not a cause?" Then he turned from him toward another and said the same thing; and these people answered him as the first ones did. Now when the words which David spoke were heard, they reported them to Saul; and he sent for him. Then David said to Saul, "Let no man's heart fail because of him; your servant will go and fight with this Philistine." And Saul said

to David, "You are not able to go against this Philistine to fight with him; for you are a youth, and he a man of war from his youth." But David said to Saul, "Your servant used to keep his father's sheep, and when a lion or a bear came and took a lamb out of the flock, I went out after it and struck it, and delivered the lamb from its mouth; and when it arose against me, I caught it by its beard, and struck and killed it. Your servant has killed both lion and bear; and this uncircumcised Philistine will be like one of them, seeing he has defied the armies of the living God." Moreover David said, "The Lord, who delivered me from the paw of the lion and from the paw of the bear, He will deliver me from the hand of this Philistine." And Saul said to David, "Go, and the Lord be with you!"

3. **1 Samuel 17:40-47** — Then he took his staff in his hand; and he chose for himself five smooth stones from the brook, and put them in a shepherd's bag, in a pouch which he had, and his sling was in his hand. And he drew near to the Philistine. So the Philistine came, and began drawing near to David, and the man who bore the shield went before him. And when the Philistine looked about and saw David, he disdained him; for he was only a youth, ruddy and good-looking. So the Philistine said to David, "Am I a dog, that you come to me with sticks?" And the Philistine cursed David by his gods. And the Philistine said to David, "Come to me, and I will give your flesh to the birds of the air and the beasts of the field!" Then David said to the Philistine, "You come to me with a sword, with a spear, and with a javelin. But I come to you in the name of the Lord of hosts, the God of the armies of Israel, whom you have defied. This day the Lord will deliver you into my hand, and I will strike you and take your head from you. And this day I will give the carcasses of the camp of the Philistines to the birds of the air and the wild beasts of the earth, that all the earth may know that there is a God in Israel. Then all this assembly shall know that the Lord does not save with sword and spear; for the battle is the Lord's, and He will give you into our hands."

SYNOPSIS

Friends, family, and authority figures may have negative opinions about you, but there is no opinion that matters more than God's. It is vital that we spend quality time with God to learn His will, His ways, and *His opinion* so we can confidently move forward in life despite what others think or say about us. When we do this, we will walk in victory over every circumstance in life.

The emphasis of this lesson:

In the Old Testament, during a time of war for Israel, a young shepherd boy overheard the threats of the opposing army, but that didn't frighten or intimidate him. David knew the opinion of God! And despite the negative opinions and lack of confidence of those around him, David pressed on with confidence in the One who had delivered him time and time again.

So far we have learned about God's unstoppable power within us that makes each of us a "joint" in the Body of Christ as well as the danger of comparison, the importance of letting go of the past, the incredible effects of forgiveness, the result of seeking God's heart and learning His opinion of us, and the power in having the courage to agree with God. God's Spirit lives in you to help you walk out all these truths in your daily life, and in this lesson, we will dive into another aspect of the great supply inside you!

When you were born again, the Holy Spirit came to live on the inside of you. He didn't come to merely visit you as if you were a hotel. No, He made His *home* in you. Then He put His resurrection power inside you, and He also put the very love of God in you. Second Timothy 1:7 says, "For God has not given us a spirit of fear, but of power and of love and of a sound mind." You have an amazing package on the inside of you. Second Corinthians 4:7 calls it a "treasure," and with this treasure, you are *unstoppable*.

Because of the power of Almighty God that resides within you, you can confidently refuse to be moved by the opinions of others. A young man in the Bible named David exemplified this so profoundly in the familiar Old Testament story we find in First Samuel 17.

David Faced the Intimidating Threats of the Enemy

In First Samuel 17:1-16, we see that the children of Israel had been under threat of the Philistine army. The Philistines were giants, and their champion named Goliath was very physically intimidating. Every day for 40 days Goliath, in all his armor, would come out to threaten and intimidate the army of Israel. And every day, the Israelite army would cower in fear of Goliath and the Philistine army.

Then in verses 17-26, we read about David, a young Hebrew shepherd boy who was approximately 17 years old. David was sent by his father Jesse into the Israelite camp to deliver food to his three older brothers who were part of the army. While David was delivering the food, he overheard Goliath's threats against the armies of Isarel. But David didn't cower in fear like so many others when he heard the giant's intimidating shouts. He had a much different reaction.

When David looked at the giant who was hurling threats of destruction at the Israelite armies, he didn't see a threatening giant. No, in David's eyes, Goliath was merely an "uncircumcised Philistine" who dared to defy the armies of the living God (*see* 1 Samuel 17:26). David was not intimidated or impressed by Goliath's words. In fact, David didn't see why the armies of Israel should be afraid at all.

When young David heard about the reward that would come to the person who could defeat the giant, he thought, *Why doesn't anyone stand up to defeat the giant?* And even though David was just a teenager, he concluded that if no one else would, *he* would be the one to step up and defeat Goliath.

David 'Turned'

Have you ever decided to take on a challenge or tried to step out in faith and accomplish something big? Were you met with supportive voices or oppositional voices saying things like, "Are you trying that again? You failed last time…," or "Who do you think you are?" Well, when David decided to take on Goliath himself, his older bother had something to say about it — and it was *not* supportive. We read about their exchange in First Samuel 17:28:

> **Now Eliab his oldest brother heard when he spoke to the men; and Eliab's anger was aroused against David, and he said, 'Why did you come down here? And with whom have you left those few sheep in the wilderness? I know your pride and the insolence of your heart, for you have come down to see the battle.'**

> And David said, 'What have I done now? Is there not a cause?' Then he [David] *turned* from him toward another and said the same thing; and these people answered him as the first ones did.

In response to his brother's comments, David didn't say, "Why aren't *you* going out to defeat the giant? Are you a wimp? Are you scared?" He didn't put his brother down or argue with his brother. Nor did he become discouraged because his brother didn't believe in him. He simply *turned*. He turned away from his brother's negative opinions and continued on with what was in his heart to do. And that's what *we* must do in the face of opposition.

When it feels like the enemy is breathing down your neck with accusations or fear, saying things like, "What are you going to do now," you must do what David did and *turn*. David didn't stay and dwell on what his brother said. Eliab said some very hurtful things to David and accused him of pride. Many of us who have been in similar situations have probably stopped to defend ourselves or have allowed hurtful words to take the wind out of our sails. But not David! He simply *turned* and moved past the opinion of his brother.

David Gained Confidence By Recounting Past Victories

The Bible continues David's story in First Samuel 17:31-33:

> Now when the words which David spoke were heard, they reported them to Saul; and he sent for him. Then David said to Saul, 'Let no man's heart fail because of him; your servant will go and fight with this Philistine.'
>
> And Saul said to David, 'You are not able to go against this Philistine to fight with him; for you are a youth, and he a man of war from his youth.'

When word reached Saul that David planned to challenge Goliath, Saul had absolutely *no* confidence in David. This opposition was different from the interaction David had with his brother because Saul flat-out told David he couldn't win. King Saul essentially said to David, "You can't do this. You're not able."

David had already received opposition from his own brother and then the King of Israel himself told him he could not win. Has anyone ever said similar things to you? Have you ever said something critical like that to *yourself*? Well, we can learn a lot from David's response to that kind of opposition.

> **But David said to Saul, 'Your servant used to keep his father's sheep, and when a lion or a bear came and took a lamb out of the flock, I went out after it and struck it, and delivered the lamb from its mouth; and when it arose against me, I caught it by its beard, and struck and killed it. Your servant has killed both lion and bear; and this uncircumcised Philistine will be like one of them, seeing he has defied the armies of the living God.' Moreover David said, 'The Lord, who delivered me from the paw of the lion and from the paw of the bear, He will deliver me from the hand of this Philistine.' And Saul said to David, 'Go, and the Lord be with you!'**
> — 1 Samuel 17:34-37

David, who is believed to have been a 17-year-old boy, stood up to the King of Israel and confidently declared how God had helped him defeat a lion and a bear while he protected his sheep. In David's mind, he had every reason to believe God would deliver him from this Philistine just as he had always done before — this was no different.

Because David was a shepherd, he spent most of his time alone in the fields and in the wilderness. As he cared for the sheep he tended, he worshiped and praised God, and over time he learned more deeply who God is and cultivated a personal relationship with Him. David got to know the mighty One who could deliver him from *any* enemy. In fact, he was so confident in who God was that as he recounted his past victories, it convinced Saul too! Saul finally said, "Go, and the Lord be with you!" (v. 37).

When David looked at Goliath, he proclaimed what he saw. But he wasn't like the Israelites who only saw a threatening giant who would destroy all of Israel's armies. No, David saw a defeated enemy who would be delivered into his hand. David had been with God, and he knew what God could do. This giant was no match for the God David had come to know in the fields and in the wilderness.

If you want to confidently stand up to negative opinions — including your own negative thoughts about yourself — you must spend time with God, getting to know Him and watching Him deliver you time and time again. And when you spend time reading and listening to the Word of God and then practice speaking it out of your mouth, your own voice will instill confidence in you. As you open your mouth and agree with the power of God on the inside of you, the same thing that happened to David will happen to you: Courage, confidence, and the ability to push past every negative opinion and prove the naysayers wrong will rise up from the supply of the Spirit that resides in your spirit.

David Used a Familiar Weapon

As David prepared to fight Goliath, King Saul put his own armor on David. But the armor didn't fit. In fact, the armor was so ill-fitting that David couldn't even walk in it. Instead, David opted to go without any armor and took only what was familiar to him — a slingshot and a few stones. Because David had confidence in how God had worked in his life before, he confidently used what was familiar to him rather than give up or try to do things Saul's way.

In the same way, when you've spent time with God and have become familiar with the way He works through *you*, you can remind yourself of all the times God has come through and then confidently step out with the assurance that God will bring you the victory. You may not be able to attack life's giants in the same way you have seen others do it, but that's okay! Be yourself and confidently and boldly confront the giants of life with the weapons God has given *you*.

Let's read the exchange between David and Goliath in First Samuel 17:44-46:

> **And the Philistine said to David, 'Come to me, and I will give your flesh to the birds of the air and the beasts of the field!' Then David said to the Philistine, 'You come to me with a sword, with a spear, and with a javelin. But I come to you in the name of the Lord of hosts, the God of the armies of Israel, whom you have defied. This day the Lord will deliver you into my hand, and I will strike you and take your head from you. And this day I will give the carcasses of the camp of the Philistines to the birds of the air and the wild beasts of the earth, that all the earth may know that there is a God in Israel.'**

Once David said these words, he took the weapon that was familiar to him — his sling and stones — and ran toward Goliath. As he ran, David slung one of the stones in his sling and hit the giant in the head where he was most vulnerable. At David's deadly strike, Goliath fell, and David took the giant's own sword and cut off Goliath's head!

Friend, the enemy will try to render you ineffective with negative thought patterns or the opposing opinions of others, but the supply of the Spirit in you empowers you to turn around and render that attack ineffective. You must *refuse* to give place to the negative opinions of others or the thoughts you have about yourself that are contrary to God's Word. Stand your ground and declare God's opinion above all others. Choose to listen to and value the only opinion that truly matter's — God's.

Remember, you have the Greater One living on the inside of you, and He's greater than *any* pressure that exists in this world. He's also the greatest Comforter and Encourager you will ever meet!

STUDY QUESTIONS

Be diligent to present yourself approved to God, a worker who does not need to be ashamed, rightly dividing the word of truth.
— 2 Timothy 2:15

1. How did David's ongoing times of prayer and worship with God as well as his past experiences with the lion and the bear build his confidence in God?
2. Read First Samuel 17:31-37. When Saul first heard about David's decision to confront Goliath, he did not have confidence that David could succeed. How did David convince King Saul of God's ability to deliver Goliath into his hands?
3. Explain why David chose a slingshot and stones over Saul's fully outfitted set of armor when he went to face Goliath.

PRACTICAL APPLICATION

But be doers of the word, and not hearers only, deceiving yourselves.
— James 1:22

1. David turned away from his older brother when he was met with a negative opinion. He did not dwell on the lack of confidence that those around him had. What do you need to "turn" away from in order to continue moving forward in your pursuit of God's will for your life?
2. As he was preparing to fight Goliath, David chose a slingshot and stones, the weapon that was most familiar to him. What weapon is most familiar to you? How has God worked through you in the past to bring about victory in your life?
3. Are you currently facing a "giant"? If not, you will likely face one eventually, as challenges come to everyone at some point. Read Psalm 77:11 and 12, Isaiah 46:9, and First Chronicles 16:12. According to these scriptures, how important is it to remember the miracles God has done in your life? Make a list of at least two instances when God delivered you out of a difficult situation and place it in an easily accessible location. Regularly remind yourself of the victories God has brought about in your life so that the next time you are faced with a "giant," you can confidently approach it with boldness and assurance that God will bring you the victory.

LESSON 8

TOPIC
Faith for a Miracle

SCRIPTURES

1. **Mark 10:46-52** — Now they came to Jericho. As He went out of Jericho with His disciples and a great multitude, blind Bartimaeus, the son of Timaeus, sat by the road begging. And when he heard that it was Jesus of Nazareth, he began to cry out and say, "Jesus, Son of David, have mercy on me!" Then many warned him to be quiet; but he cried out all the more, "Son of David, have mercy on me!" So Jesus stood still and commanded him to be called. Then they called the blind man, saying to him, "Be of good cheer. Rise, He is calling you." And throwing aside his garment, he rose and came to Jesus. So Jesus answered and said to him, "What do you want Me to do for you?" The blind man said to Him, "Rabboni, that I may receive my sight." Then

Jesus said to him, Go your way; your faith has made you well." And immediately he received his sight and followed Jesus on the road.

SYNOPSIS

Have you ever faced discouragement when you dared to believe God for a miracle? Maybe people around you said things like, "Why would you believe God for that?" or, "You should just give up!" Well, God has a different opinion. He wants you to push past the unbelief of those around you and, instead, agree with the powerful supply that is *in* you!

The emphasis of this lesson:

When Jesus walked the earth, He did many miracles. And after hearing about the wonderful things Christ did, a blind beggar named Bartimaeus was determined to receive one of those miracles for himself — regardless of what the people around him said.

In previous lessons, we have learned about God's unstoppable power within us that makes us each a "joint" in the Body of Christ. We also learned about the danger of comparison, the importance of letting go of the past, the incredible force of forgiveness, the need to seek God's heart and learn His opinion, and the power in having the courage to agree with God. God's Spirit lives in you to help you walk out all these truths in your daily life, and in this lesson, we will dive into another aspect of the supernatural supply inside you!

God chose you before the foundations of the world. He saw you, knew you, gave you a purpose, made a plan for your life, and put His mighty Spirit on the inside of you when you were born again so you could fulfill that plan. The mighty power of God on the inside of you is greater than any pressure that would try to get you off course, which means *unstoppable* power lives in you! Remember these truths as we uncover what unstoppable faith looks like when it is released from the supply of God.

The Blind Man Who Heard of Jesus

Let's dive into the story of an unstoppable man named Bartimaeus. His story begins in Mark 10:46:

> Now they came to Jericho. As He went out of Jericho with His disciples and a great multitude, blind Bartimaeus, the son of Timaeus, sat by the road begging.

Bartimaeus was totally blind, and he lived a very discouraging life. Part of his daily routine was to sit by the road begging people for money, and according to the customs of the time, he would have been required to wear certain clothes that identified him as a beggar and a blind man. He did not live a privileged life like many do today. Think of all the things that we take for granted like eyesight, a bed, and clean clothes. For instance, you are using your eyes to read this study guide right now! Bartimaeus was not so privileged; his was a life of poverty and discouragement.

Because Bartimaeus sat by the road every day, he likely overheard many different conversations of passersby. It would be reasonable to assume that over the course of his days sitting by the road, Bartimaeus had previously heard about Jesus and the miracles He had performed for others. That would explain why when he heard that Jesus was coming his way, he got very excited. Something was about to change in his life. It seems that Bartimaeus knew Jesus of Nazareth had something that he needed, so he began to cry out to Him.

What To Do When Doubt and Unbelief Surround You

The story continues in verse 47:

> And when he heard that it was Jesus of Nazareth, he began to cry out and say, 'Jesus, Son of David, have mercy on me!' Then many warned him to be quiet; but he cried out all the more, 'Son of David, have mercy on me!'

Imagine for a moment the scene that was unfolding. Blind Bartimaeus was sitting by the road, likely holding a cup to collect the little bit of money he could from generous people who took pity on him. And as he sat in his dirty beggar's clothes, unable to see, he eagerly waited for Jesus to come his way. When he heard that Jesus was close by, he began crying out, "Jesus, Son of David, have mercy on me!"

But immediately after Bartimaeus began crying out to Jesus, the people around him told him to be quiet. They essentially said, "Shut up! You don't need to do that. Why are you screaming?" And, according to Bible scholars and commentators, the people didn't just tell him one time to be quiet — they rebuked him repeatedly.

Has anyone ever told you to be quiet when you were crying out to God? It may not have been quite as blatant as the people who tried to silence Bartimaeus, but it may have come in the form of negative opinions. Maybe someone said something like, "Why are you calling on God? Why don't you just give up?" Sometimes when we dare to believe God, we find ourselves surrounded by doubt and unbelief.

On the program, Denise shared a story of a woman she met many years ago who had multiple sclerosis. This woman was blind in one eye, and she was paralyzed on the other side of her body. She believed that Jesus was the healer, and she began to confess and believe His Word. She made sure that her ears heard the Word of God about healing 24 hours a day. But, unfortunately, some of her relatives and the people around her began saying things like, "Why is she believing God? We need to plan her funeral," and, "Is she crazy? There's no help for her in God."

So what should we do when this happens? We read about how David faced people who spoke similar negative, unbelieving things to him and about him when he dared to believe God to help him defeat Goliath. And when blind Bartimaeus began to boldly cry out to Jesus for mercy, he was met with the same unbelief too. For Bartimaeus, though, it wasn't just one person offering a negative opinion. Multiple people around him tried to silence him by repeatedly telling him to be quiet and give up. But according to Mark 10:47, when Bartimaeus heard the people's rebukes, he cried out *all the more* — and it got Jesus' attention.

A New Identity in Christ

Jesus saw something in Bartimaeus, and it wasn't simply because he was yelling loudly. Jesus saw *faith*. Mark 10:49 says, "So Jesus stood still and commanded him to be called…." Can you imagine how Bartimaeus felt when Jesus called for him? He must have been *so excited*! And Verse 49 goes on to tell us something else amazing. Once Jesus stopped and called for Bartimaeus, the crowd around him suddenly began to say: "…Be of good cheer. Rise, He is calling you."

The very same people who rebuked Bartimaeus just moments earlier began encouraging him! What does this tell us? It tells us that sometimes the people around us who offer negative opinions aren't really trying to help us. This isn't the case for all people; some people do mean well, but many don't care about us or our situation at all. They are simply living in the excitement of the moment. The people in this story easily went from telling Bartimaeus to shut up to encouraging him to be of good cheer. They didn't truly care for him or understand what he was going through. But Jesus was touched by Bartimaeus's faith, and He did care about what he was going through.

It's the same for us today. When we use our faith and believe God's Word, we agree with the power of God. And just like Bartimaeus did, we can touch Jesus' heart with our faith. And just like Bartimaeus did, we can receive a miracle that will change our life forever!

Mark 10:50 says, "And throwing aside his garment, he [Bartimaeus] rose and came to Jesus." The garment Bartimaeus threw off was the garment that identified him as a blind man and a beggar. When he wore that garment, it identified him as someone to be pitied and someone who needed support. It made people feel sorry for him. This garment enabled him to collect money from generous people every day so he could continue to live. But he threw the garment aside and went to Jesus!

By throwing his beggar's garment aside, Bartimaeus rejected his old identity. It was as if he was saying, "Soon I will not be blind anymore! I will not be a beggar anymore. I have been called by *Jesus*!" Then in verse 51, we read, "So Jesus answered and said to him, 'What do you want Me to do for you?'"

You may be thinking, *Why would Jesus ask Bartimaeus that question? He was blind. Wasn't it obvious what he wanted?* But Jesus wanted him to vocalize exactly what he was asking Jesus to do. Bartimaeus was a beggar; he'd spent his days sitting by the road, asking people for money. He could have been calling out to Jesus to ask Him for money too. Maybe Jesus wanted to hear Bartimaeus say out of his mouth that he was not asking for money and that he was asking to be *healed*.

But Bartimaeus was not asking for money. He did not want a temporary solution that would make things better only for a time or to continue living the same life he'd been living. He did not ask for a "quick fix" that would allow him to continue receiving pity from the generous people in the city. No, Bartimaeus wanted a *miracle*!

Verse 51 continues, "…The blind man said to Him, 'Rabboni, that I may receive my sight.'" Bartimaeus knew *exactly* what he wanted. He wanted the miracle-working power that he knew Jesus had for him. He wanted a new life; he wanted Jesus to open his eyes! And verse 52 says, "Then Jesus said to him, 'Go your way; your faith has made you well.' And immediately he received his sight and followed Jesus on the road."

Following Jesus and Agreeing With God

Blind Bartimaeus was not blind anymore! Because of his new eyesight, he was able to follow Jesus and live the new life he had been given. Bartimaeus would now be able to leave behind the life of begging and participate in society and get a job to support himself. Before this encounter, he could never have followed Jesus on the road. What an incredible testimony of the power of pushing past the negative opinions of others.

On the program, Denise shared the following excerpt from her book *Unstoppable*:

> The devil will use anything to try to keep us boxed inside a negative label, because he's so afraid of the divine supply inside us. He knows that God intends to use our supply mightily to help set people free! So I want to get this thought firmly planted in your heart: Any negative label that the enemy has tried to put on you, whether as a child or as an adult, is *not* the truth. What you are to believe about yourself is what *God* says about you.
>
> - God says about you that you are more than a conqueror (*see* Romans 8:37).
> - God says about you that you have not received the spirit of fear, but of power, love, and a sound mind (*see* 2 Timothy 1:7).
> - God says about you that you are not rejected; rather, you are accepted in the Beloved (*see* Ephesians 1:6).
> - God says about you that your name is written on the palm of His hand (*see* Isaiah 49:16).
> - God says about you that greater is He who is in you than he that is in the world (*see* 1 John 4:4).
>
> These are the true labels that should be written on the "monogrammed T-shirt" that we wear over our souls! It's what *God* says about us. It's not what a parent said. It's not what a spouse said.

It's not what a friend said. It's not what a boss said. [It's what God said — *and says* — about you.]

Friend, if we listen to what God says about us and agree with it, we agree with the supply of His power that is on the inside of us. And as we agree and identify with His power, we will see God move powerfully on our behalf and totally change our lives for the better!

STUDY QUESTIONS

> Be diligent to present yourself approved to God, a worker who does not need to be ashamed, rightly dividing the word of truth.
> — 2 Timothy 2:15

1. Explain the significance of Bartimaeus' throwing aside his beggar's garment. How does this action reflect his faith and readiness for a new identity in Christ?
2. The crowd surrounding Bartimaeus changed what they were saying after Jesus singled Bartimaeus out among them. What does this tell us about the opinions of others?
3. Based on what you know about Bartimaeus and the culture of the time, why do you think Jesus asked Bartimaeus what he wanted Him to do for him?

PRACTICAL APPLICATION

> But be doers of the word, and not hearers only, deceiving yourselves.
> —James 1:22

1. After being a beggar for so long, Bartimaeus rejected his old identity by throwing off his beggar's garment. Are there any "garments" or labels from your past that you need to throw aside to fully embrace who God says you are?
2. Bartimaeus had heard of Jesus' miracles for others and believed Jesus would heal him too. How does remembering what God has done for other people help inspire faith in you for your own miracle?
3. When Bartimaeus was healed, he received not just a temporary solution, but a life-changing miracle. Are there areas where you've settled

for temporary fixes rather than seeking the deeper, lasting transformation God offers?

LESSON 9

TOPIC
It Is Well

SCRIPTURES
1. **2 Kings 4:11-37** — And it happened one day that he came there, and he turned in to the upper room and lay down there. Then he said to Gehazi his servant, "Call this Shunammite woman." When he had called her, she stood before him. And he said to him, "Say now to her, 'Look, you have been concerned for us with all this care. What can I do for you? Do you want me to speak on your behalf to the king or to the commander of the army?" She answered, "I dwell among my own people." So he said, "What then is to be done for her?" And Gehazi answered, "Actually, she has no son, and her husband is old." So he said, "Call her." When he had called her, she stood in the doorway. Then he said, "About this time next year you shall embrace a son." And she said, "No, my lord. Man of God, do not lie to your maidservant!" But the woman conceived, and bore a son when the appointed time had come, of which Elisha had told her. And the child grew. Now it happened one day that he went out to his father, to the reapers. And he said to his father, "My head, my head!" So he said to a servant, "Carry him to his mother." When he had taken him and brought him to his mother, he sat on her knees till noon, and then died. And she went up and laid him on the bed of the man of God, shut the door upon him, and went out. Then she called to her husband, and said, "Please send me one of the young men and one of the donkeys, that I may run to the man of God and come back." So he said, "Why are you going to him today? It is neither the New Moon nor the Sabbath." And she said, "It is well." Then she saddled a donkey, and said to her servant, "Drive, and go forward; do not slacken the pace for me unless I tell you." And so she departed, and went to the man of God at Mount Carmel. So it was, when the man of God saw her afar off, that he said to his servant Gehazi, "Look, the Shunammite woman!

Please run now to meet her, and say to her, 'Is it well with you? Is it well with your husband? Is it well with the child?'" And she answered, "It is well." Now when she came to the man of God at the hill, she caught him by the feet, but Gehazi came near to push her away. But the man of God said, "Let her alone; for her soul is in deep distress, and the Lord has hidden it from me, and has not told me." So she said, "Did I ask a son of my lord? Did I not say, 'Do not deceive me'?" Then he said to Gehazi, "Get yourself ready, and take my staff in your hand, and be on your way. If you meet anyone, do not greet him; and if anyone greets you, do not answer him; but lay my staff on the face of the child." And the mother of the child said, "As the Lord lives, and as your soul lives, I will not leave you." So he arose and followed her. Now Gehazi went on ahead of them, and laid the staff on the face of the child; but there was neither voice nor hearing. Therefore he went back to meet him, and told him, saying, "The child has not awakened." When Elisha came into the house, there was the child, lying dead on his bed. He went in therefore, shut the door behind the two of them, and prayed to the Lord. And he went up and lay on the child, and put his mouth on his mouth, his eyes on his eyes, and his hands on his hands; and he stretched himself out on the child, and the flesh of the child became warm. He returned and walked back and forth in the house, and again went up and stretched himself out on him; then the child sneezed seven times, and the child opened his eyes. And he called Gehazi and said, "Call this Shunammite woman." So he called her. And when she came in to him, he said, "Pick up your son." So she went in, fell at his feet, and bowed to the ground; then she picked up her son and went out.

SYNOPSIS

When we are faced with an impossible situation, we always have a choice to make: Will we keep our eyes trained on God and believe His promise, or will we sink into despair with our eyes focused only on the problem? It is perfectly normal to become emotional during hard times, but the supernatural supply inside you enables you to say, "It is well," even when everything around you seems hopeless.

You may have to push through some very difficult circumstances, but when you reach the other side of that difficulty, you will see that it was worth it to witness what God can do to turn things around. When you agree with that unstoppable power that is in you by the Holy Spirit and you push past fear and offense and the negative opinions of others, you *will* see victory in your life!

The emphasis of this lesson:

A Shunammite woman was given a promise from God. And when the enemy tried to rob her of that promise, she refused to settle for anything less than a miracle! Her example shows us that we can draw from our supply and push through impossible situations, just like she did, until we see victory in our lives.

In previous lessons, we have learned about God's unstoppable power within us that makes us each a "joint" in the Body of Christ. We've also seen the danger of comparison, the importance of letting go of the past, the incredible force of forgiveness, how to seek God's heart and learn His opinion, the power in having the courage to agree with God, and how being bold enough to expect a miracle touches the heart of Jesus. God's Spirit lives in us to help us walk out these truths in our daily lives, and in this lesson, we will learn about a woman who pushed through a very impossible situation in order to see her victory.

A Promise for the Shunammite Woman

In Second Kings 4, we read about the prophet Elisha who was being used mightily by God. The Bible also tells us a Shunammite woman, who had likely heard about Elisha and the amazing works God was doing through him, persuaded Elisha to let her prepare some food for him. It then goes on to say that as often as he passed by her house, he would stop there to eat, and one day this woman told her husband that she had a desire to do something nice for Elisha. She wanted to build a special room for him in their home. She had the whole design planned out: a table, a lamp, a chair, and a bed. She wanted the room to be comfortable for him.

Later when Elisha came through her city, he and his servant stayed with the Shunammite woman and her husband.

> **And it happened one day that he [Elisha] came there, and he turned in to the upper room and lay down there. Then he said to Gehazi his servant, 'Call this Shunammite woman.' When he had called her, she stood before him. And he said to him, 'Say now to her, "Look, you have been concerned for us with all**

this care. What can I do for you? Do you want me to speak on your behalf to the king or to the commander of the army?" She answered, 'I dwell among my own people.' So he said, 'What then is to be done for her ?' And Gehazi answered, 'Actually, she has no son, and her husband is old.' So he said, 'Call her.' When he had called her, she stood in the doorway. Then he said, 'About this time next year you shall embrace a son.' And she said, 'No, my lord. Man of God, do not lie to your maidservant!' But the woman conceived, and bore a son when the appointed time had come, of which Elisha had told her. And the child grew....

— 2 Kings 4:11-18

Elisha so enjoyed his stay and was so grateful to this woman that he asked his servant Gehazi how he might show his gratitude to her. Gehazi let him know that the woman's husband was advanced in years and they had no son. Elisha prophesied that she would give birth to a son the following year. And then *it happened*, and the child grew.

'It Is Well'

Second Kings 4:18-20 says that one day, the child was out with his father, and something tragic happened:

> ...Now it happened one day that he went out to his father, to the reapers. And he said to his father, 'My head, my head!' So he said to a servant, 'Carry him to his mother.' When he had taken him and brought him to his mother, he sat on her knees till noon, and then died.

Can you imagine the pain this woman must have felt? Her only son, her miracle boy, had just died in her arms. But instead of planning a funeral, the Shunammite woman started planning a *resurrection*. Verse 21 says, "And she went up and laid him on the bed of the man of God, shut the door upon him, and went out." The man of God, Elisha, was no longer in her home. He was *long* gone. The best she could do was place her dead son on the bed where Elisha had once slept and *shut the door*.

Any other mother probably would have wanted to hold her son and mourn his death. But rather than plan a funeral, she put her dead son as close to the power of God as she could, which was the bed of the prophet.

Verses 22 and 23 tell us what happened next:

> Then she called to her husband, and said, 'Please send me one of the young men and one of the donkeys, that I may run to the man of God and come back.' So he said, 'Why are you going to him today? It is neither the New Moon nor the Sabbath.' And she said, 'It is well.'

The woman didn't inform her husband that his son had died. All she said was, "It is well." Naturally speaking, things were anything *but* well! Her dead son was lying in the prophet's bed. But she chose to say, "It is well."

> Then she saddled a donkey, and said to her servant, 'Drive, and go forward; do not slacken the pace for me unless I tell you.' And so she departed, and went to the man of God at Mount Carmel. So it was, when the man of God saw her afar off, that he said to his servant Gehazi, 'Look, the Shunammite woman! Please run now to meet her, and say to her, "Is it well with you? Is it well with your husband? Is it well with the child?"' And she answered, 'It is well.'
>
> — 2 Kings 4:24,25

Every time she was asked about the state of things, she responded with, "It is well." She pushed past every emotion and despair-filled thought that tried to come to her mind. With every response of "It is well," she proclaimed that her son would live again.

Friend, when we are faced with impossible circumstances, it matters what comes out of our mouth. We shouldn't allow ourselves to say things like, "It's not going to work out," or "I probably won't get what I need from God." We must not allow ourselves to dwell on the problem or start talking about how bad things are. No, we must believe what God has spoken and like the Shunammite woman, say, "It is well," no matter what the situation looks like.

A Miraculous Recovery

On the program, Denise shared the story of a body builder she knew who was in a horrible car accident that left him with a broken back. The doctors said he would never walk again and that he would be living in a wheelchair for the rest of his life. He was paralyzed.

The man's wife came to him and said, "Honey, you know what we believe. You know what we preach. You've got to stand up to this." And that man — with all the contraptions attached to his body that were literally holding him together — said out of his mouth, "It is well."

Eventually, that man was miraculously healed. Since then, he has returned to body building, and he has preached in many different nations about the power of God. The man experienced the power of God because he did not focus on the situation, he kept his eyes on God. He was looking at the resurrection power of the Holy Spirit on the inside of him to resurrect his crippled body. And as he identified with the power of God and said, "It is well," God's power came over that man and completely healed him. That is the power of agreeing with the truth of God's Word and the supply of power inside you!

Never Let Go of Your Promise

The Shunammite woman's story continues in Second Kings 4:27-30:

> **Now when she came to the man of God at the hill, she caught him by the feet, but Gehazi came near to push her away. But the man of God said, 'Let her alone; for her soul is in deep distress, and the Lord has hidden it from me, and has not told me.' So she said, 'Did I ask a son of my lord? Did I not say, "Do not deceive me"?' Then he said to Gehazi, 'Get yourself ready, and take my staff in your hand, and be on your way. If you meet anyone, do not greet him; and if anyone greets you, do not answer him; but lay my staff on the face of the child.' And the mother of the child said, 'As the Lord lives, and as your soul lives, I will not leave you.' So he arose and followed her.**

This was one convicted and determined woman! She ignored the rejection of Gehazi who tried to push her away. The Shunammite woman would not settle for anything less than a miracle from God.

Verses 31-37 tell of the incredible miracle the woman received:

> **Now Gehazi went on ahead of them, and laid the staff on the face of the child; but there was neither voice nor hearing. Therefore he went back to meet him, and told him, saying, 'The child has not awakened.' When Elisha came into the house, there was the child, lying dead on his bed. He went in therefore,**

shut the door behind the two of them, and prayed to the Lord. And he went up and lay on the child, and put his mouth on his mouth, his eyes on his eyes, and his hands on his hands; and he stretched himself out on the child, and the flesh of the child became warm. He returned and walked back and forth in the house, and again went up and stretched himself out on him; then the child sneezed seven times, and the child opened his eyes. And he called Gehazi and said, 'Call this Shunammite woman.' So he called her. And when she came in to him, he said, "Pick up your son." So she went in, fell at his feet, and bowed to the ground; then she picked up her son and went out.

Wow! The Shunammite woman believed God despite her seemingly impossible circumstances and saw God's faithfulness. She held on to the Word of God and did not allow what she saw to stop or discourage her from chasing after the promise she had been given. She didn't even allow other people to cause her to let go of the promise. And as a result, she saw the incredible power of God on display to bring His will to pass in her life.

On the program, Denise read an excerpt from her book *Unstoppable*:

> I want you to see what this Shunammite woman was like. She'd already experienced one miracle when her son was born, so she had that encouragement. But she'd never heard of anyone else being raised from the dead. She couldn't say, 'Oh, I heard about this person and that person who were raised from the dead!' No one was being raised from the dead in the land.
>
> Nevertheless, this woman believed that way! Holding her dead son, she was thinking, *I'm not losing him. I've had one miracle. I'm going to have another miracle!*
>
> This mother was not planning on the worst outcome. She was planning on the *ultimate best* outcome. And she *immediately* went into action — not to plan a funeral, but to prepare for the resurrection of her dead son!

We live in a time when there are so many reasons for heartaches and sleepless nights. But when it looks like we've experienced the death of our God-given dream because of difficult circumstances or people's opinions, we need the faith to think like the Shunammite woman did in her impossible situation.

You may be thinking, *Oh, that's just a story* or *The child had to be resurrected so the story could be included in the Bible.* But friend, the Shunammite woman was a *real* woman who had just lost her *real* son as she held him in her lap. And in that moment of pain and loss, she had a choice to make. It would have been perfectly normal for her to break down and sink into mourning and grief. Yet despite the wave of emotions that likely assaulted her mind, and instead of planning a funeral, she began planning a *resurrection*!

STUDY QUESTIONS

> Be diligent to present yourself approved to God, a worker
> who does not need to be ashamed, rightly dividing the word of truth.
> — 2 Timothy 2:15

1. Explain the importance of the phrase "It is well" in the Shunammite woman's response to her son's death. What does her choice to respond with only this phrase reveal about her level of trust in God's promise?
2. Once the Shunammite woman had grabbed hold of Elisha's feet, as we read in verse 27, she refused to let go unless he agreed to come with her in person. Compare Gehazi's response to this woman's faith with that of Elisha. What are some important differences?

PRACTICAL APPLICATION

> But be doers of the word,
> and not hearers only, deceiving yourselves.
> — James 1:22

1. Take a moment to reflect on your God-given dreams. Have you loosened your grip of faith on something God has spoken to you? If so, what can you do to stir your faith again to see that dream come to pass? If not, what is one verse you can speak to yourself to fortify your faith concerning that dream?
2. Be honest with yourself: When you face difficult situations, what is your first response? Do you dwell on the impossibility of things and speak negatively about your circumstances, or do you run to the Word of God and speak His promises? What life changes will you make today to ensure you always speak the Word of God, no matter how hopeless things may seem?

LESSON 10

TOPIC
A Greater Purpose

SCRIPTURES

1. **Mark 14:3-9** — And being in Bethany at the house of Simon the leper, as He sat at the table, a woman came having an alabaster flask of very costly oil of spikenard. Then she broke the flask and poured it on His head. But there were some who were indignant among themselves, and said, "Why was this fragrant oil wasted? For it might have been sold for more than three hundred denarii and given to the poor." And they criticized her sharply. But Jesus said, "Let her alone. Why do you trouble her? She has done a good work for Me. For you have the poor with you always, and whenever you wish you may do them good; but Me you do not have always. She has done what she could. She has come beforehand to anoint My body for burial. Assuredly, I say to you, wherever this gospel is preached in the whole world, what this woman has done will also be told as a memorial to her."

SYNOPSIS

Over these past several lessons, we have learned about God's unstoppable power within us that makes us each a "joint" in the Body of Christ as well as the danger of comparison, the importance of letting go of the past, the incredible force of forgiveness, how to seek God's heart and learn His opinion, the power in having the courage to agree with God, how to touch the heart of Jesus, and how to say, "It is well" when we're facing devastating circumstances. God's Spirit lives in us to help us walk out these truths in our daily life, and He is waiting on us to draw on His help and begin to give out of the supernatural supply that is in us.

There will be a day when we each stand before God, and on that day, we will all want to hear Him say to us, "Well done My good and faithful servant," (*see* Matthew 25:14-30). So until that day comes, we must do well! We must not allow things like fear, offense, or the negative opinions of other people to become obstacles that stop us from doing all that the Lord asks of us. Everything we do, whether in worship to God or in service of another, is valuable to Him, and Jesus even calls these acts "good works." As we will see in today's example, when we give what we can out of our supply, Jesus commends us! He treasures everything that we bring as an offering to Him.

The emphasis of this lesson:

An ordinary woman woke up one day with a desire to worship Jesus and pour her love on Him, but to her surprise, she was met with anger, hostility, and criticism. Despite the indignant protests from those around her, this woman pressed on and worshiped Jesus anyway. This extraordinary act of love reveals the true value Jesus places on what we give out of our supply and encourages us to do the same.

A Costly Gift

And being in Bethany at the house of Simon the leper, as He [Jesus] sat at the table, a woman came having an alabaster flask of very costly oil of spikenard. Then she broke the flask and poured it on His head.
— Mark 14:3-9

In Mark chapter 14, we read about a woman who broke a flask of oil over Jesus' head. What she did may not seem noteworthy, but the value of the oil that she poured on Jesus was about 300 denarii, which was the sum of more than one year's wages! Can you imagine using more than your entire year's salary to purchase a single flask of oil, only to pour it onto someone else? That's exactly what this woman did. When she broke the alabaster flask, it and its contents were gone, never to be used again — but that was her intention. Her plan was to give this valuable offering in its entirety to Jesus.

This woman was quite brave because as she walked up to Jesus, she also came into the company of several men who were lying down and leisurely enjoying their lunch. It was very unusual for a woman to interrupt this type of gathering according to the customs of that time. But regardless, she entered the room, walked directly up to Jesus, broke her flask, and began to pour every drop of the perfumed oil upon His head.

Verse 4 tells us, "But there were some who were indignant among themselves, and said, 'Why was this fragrant oil wasted?'" Those who voiced their opinions were not simply whispering to each other. The original text indicates that they sternly rebuked her. Some Bible scholars and commentators even say that these angry men gave her nasty looks of disdain. They were truly offended by her act of worship.

Because of the great value of the oil the woman brought, the offended men essentially thought she was stupid; they assumed she didn't know what she was wasting. We can reasonably assume that this was what the men were thinking because Mark 14:5 says they ridiculed her, saying, "'For it might have been sold for more than three hundred denarii and given to the poor.' And they criticized her sharply."

A 'Good Work'

All this woman wanted to do was worship Jesus, but she was criticized for her actions. We must learn from this example and make the decision to never ever criticize another person's act of worship! No matter how we feel, we should always cheer on and champion anyone who has a desire to pour out his or her love on Jesus, even if it looks frivolous or wasteful to us. And we should pour out our love on Him too! Do everything you can to worship and serve the Lord.

And in verse 6, we see that Jesus loved this woman's gift!

> **But Jesus said, 'Let her alone. Why do you trouble her? She has done a good work for Me.'**

There are three instances in the Bible when either Jesus or a man of God said to someone, "Let her alone." Each time, it was said in defense of a person who was reaching out to God in faith. We saw one of these examples in our last lesson with the Shunammite woman and Elisha. When the woman grabbed hold of Elisha's feet, his servant Gehazi tried to stop her, but Elisha said to him, "Let her alone" (*see* 2 Kings 4:27).

This tells us that God wants us to seek Him and worship Him no matter what the people around us do or say. It also shows us that if anyone comes against us while we are trying to seek God, our Lord will come to our defense. In fact, Jesus went on in Mark 14:7 and 8 to address the angry men further, saying, "For you have the poor with you always, and whenever you wish you may do them good; but Me you do not have always. She has done what she could...."

Jesus commended this woman who defied cultural norms to worship Him, and He made two important statements. He said she had done "a good work" (v. 6) and that she did "what she could" (v. 8). This woman might not have done anything that seemed noteworthy or logical to those men, but Jesus saw the value in what she did and what she gave. He defended her, saying she did good and that she did what she could. Jesus doesn't commend us for doing what we can't; He commends us for doing *what we can*. And when we do, He calls it a "good work." *Wow!*

But that wasn't all Jesus had to say. Without realizing it, the woman had done something *monumental*. Jesus explains this in verses 8 and 9, which says, "…She has come beforehand to anoint My body for burial. Assuredly, I say to you, wherever this gospel is preached in the whole world, what this woman has done will also be told as a memorial to her."

This woman had no idea she was changing history or that she was anointing the Lamb of God who would take away the sins of the world. When she went to sleep the night before, she was not thinking she would wake up the next day and play a pivotal role in the most significant event in the history of mankind. She was simply acting on her love for Jesus and her desire to worship Him in the best way she knew how. And as a result, her act of worship has been talked about for more than 2,000 years! *That is incredible!*

On the program, Denise shared this excerpt from her book *Unstoppable*:

> [The woman] didn't know that she was fulfilling a higher purpose in her act of love toward Jesus. She was just pouring out that oil, giving lavishly to Jesus out of her heart for Him. But in doing so, [the woman] actually gave out of her supply, and Jesus commended her for it.

Don't ever think that what you have to give is not enough. Whether you are teaching children at church or repeatedly extending forgiveness to the same person for the same offense, you are giving of your supply and pouring it out upon Jesus. In Matthew 25:40, Jesus said, "Assuredly, I say to you, inasmuch as you did it to one of the least of these My brethren, you did it to Me." Jesus loves and values when we give of our supply — no matter how big, small, silly, or sensible it may seem to others.

The Place Between Your Challenge and Your Miracle

There are some significant similarities between this woman's story and the story of many others in the Bible. When she woke up that morning, she was just an ordinary woman with a desire to worship Jesus. But when she went to bed that night, she went to bed as someone who had made history, as God had used her simple act of love to serve His greater purpose. She experienced two very real, yet different realities. Between these two realities, there was a place that was just as real: it was the place of *faith*.

Let's review some of the stories we've discussed in this series as well as a few others to identify their starting place, their miracle, and their place of faith:

- **Blind Bartimaeus (*see* Mark 10:46-52)** — The day Bartimaeus' life was changed, he woke up blind just like every other day before. But when he went to bed that night, he could see. The place between these two realities was *the place of faith*.

- **The Woman With the Issue of Blood (*see* Mark 5:25-24)** — This woman was *very* sick for 12 years — that's 4,380 mornings of waking up sick. But the evening after she met Jesus, she went to bed healed, whole, and at peace. The time she spent sick was one reality, and the moment she received her miracle was a reality too. But the time between these two was also a reality; it was *the place of faith*.

- **The Shunammite Woman (*see* 2 Kings 4:8-37)** — This courageous woman held her dead son in her lap one moment, and a few moments later, she held her live son. The fact that she held her dead son in her lap was one reality. And holding her live son in her arms was also a reality. But the place between her two realities was *the place of faith*.

- **David the Shepherd (*see* 1 Samuel 17)** — David woke up one morning as a normal shepherd boy, ready to deliver food to his brothers. But he went to bed that night a giant-killer. What occurred between the time when David overheard the giant's threats and the moment he later held Goliath's head in his hand? The answer is *the place of faith*.

- **Denise Renner** — On the program, Denise shared her own testimony of healing, when she understood that Jesus' sacrifice on the Cross not only paid for her salvation but also her healing (*see* 1 Peter 2:24). She went to bed one night with a horrible skin disease on her face and neck that she'd had for 13 years. And the next morning, she woke up completely healed. What was between those two realities? It was her *place of faith*!

We read about many notable miracles God performed in the Bible, and there are even more testimonies of God's incredible miracles for people today. He has not changed! Jesus is the same yesterday, today, and forever (*see* Hebrews 13:8). And although your problems are real, the miracle you are waiting for is also real. And, friend, there is a place where you can receive *your* miracle from God — it is in *the place of faith*!

STUDY QUESTIONS

> Be diligent to present yourself approved to God, a worker
> who does not need to be ashamed, rightly dividing the word of truth.
> — 2 Timothy 2:15

1. Read Mark 14:3-9. When the woman broke her alabaster flask and poured the expensive oil on Jesus, she caused quite a stir among some of the men present. What was Jesus' response? How do you think Jesus' words and actions might have made the woman feel while she was in the presence of her critics?

2. What does Jesus' response to the woman's bold act of worship reveal about His thoughts toward anyone who comes to Him? Are there other instances in Scripture where Jesus stands up for someone whom others are trying to turn away?

3. What do the stories of the woman with the alabaster flask, the Shunammite woman, and young David all have in common?

PRACTICAL APPLICATION

> But be doers of the word,
> and not hearers only, deceiving yourselves.
> — James 1:22

1. Think of a time when you felt led to do something for God but hesitated due to fear or the opinions of others. Did you overcome those obstacles? If so, how? If not, what would you have done differently?

2. Is there an area of your life where you feel inadequate or as though what you have to offer God isn't enough? How does what you have learned in this lesson challenge that mindset and affect how you will think from now on? What changes will you make that reflect your new perspective?
3. What would your life look like if you poured out everything you have to God? How can you show your love and devotion to Him in this current season of your life with joy and without reservation?
4. What can you do to ensure you stay in the "place of faith" during times of difficulty? How can this help you maintain hope for the miracle you need?

A Prayer To Receive Salvation

If you've never received Jesus as your Savior and Lord, now is the time for you to experience the new life Jesus wants to give you! To receive God's gift of salvation that can be obtained through Jesus alone, pray this prayer from your heart:

> *Jesus, I repent of my sin and receive You as my Savior and Lord. Wash away my sin with Your precious blood and make me completely new. I thank You that my sin is removed, and Satan no longer has any right to lay claim on me. Through Your empowering grace, I faithfully promise that I will serve You as my Lord for the rest of my life.*

If you just prayed this prayer of salvation, you are born again! You are a brand-new creation in Christ! Would you please let us know of your decision by going to **renner.org/salvation**? We would love to connect with you and pray for you as you begin your new life in Christ.

Scriptures for further study: John 3:16; John 14:6; Acts 4:12; Ephesians 1:7; Hebrews 10:19,20; 1 Peter 1:18,19; Romans 10:9,10; Colossians 1:13; 2 Corinthians 5:17; Romans 6:4; 1 Peter 1:3

Notes

CLAIM YOUR FREE RESOURCE!

As a way of introducing you further to the teaching ministry of Rick Renner, we would like to send you FREE of charge his teaching, "How To Receive a Miraculous Touch From God" on CD or as an MP3 download.

In His earthly ministry, Jesus commonly healed *all* who were sick of *all* their diseases. In this profound message, learn about the manifold dimensions of Christ's wisdom, goodness, power, and love toward all humanity who came to Him in faith with their needs.

☑ YES, I want to receive Rick Renner's monthly teaching letter!

Simply scan the QR code to claim this resource or go to:
renner.org/claim-your-free-offer

WITH US!

renner.org

- facebook.com/rickrenner • facebook.com/rennerdenise
- youtube.com/rennerministries • youtube.com/deniserenner
- instagram.com/rickrrenner • instagram.com/rennerministries_
  instagram.com/rennerdenise

www.ingramcontent.com/pod-product-compliance
Lightning Source LLC
Chambersburg PA
CBHW071627040426
42452CB00009B/1519